THE PERFECT FIT

Jackie Rutan
is a Clothing Construction Specialist and is
Director of the Sakowitz Sewing Seminars in
Houston, Texas.

THE PERFECT FIT
Easy Pattern Alterations

Jackie Rutan

PRENTICE-HALL, INC., Englewood Cliffs, New Jersey 07632

Library of Congress Cataloging in Publication Data

Rutan, Jackie.
  The perfect fit.

  (The Creative handcrafts series) (A Spectrum Book)
  Includes index.
  1. Dressmaking—Pattern design. 2. Tailoring
(Women's) I. Title.
TT520.R954   646.4 '3   76-58507
ISBN 0-13-657064-X
ISBN 0-13-657056-9 pbk.

Illustrations by Robert F. Krueger and Jackie Rutan.

© 1977 by Prentice-Hall, Inc., Englewood Cliffs, N.J. 07632

A Spectrum Book

Printed in the United States of America

10   9   8   7   6   5   4   3   2   1

PRENTICE—HALL INTERNATIONAL, INC., *London*
PRENTICE—HALL OF AUSTRALIA PTY. LIMITED, *Sydney*
PRENTICE—HALL OF CANADA, LTD., *Toronto*
PRENTICE—HALL OF INDIA PRIVATE LIMITED, *New Delhi*
PRENTICE—HALL OF JAPAN, INC., *Tokyo*
PRENTICE—HALL OF SOUTHEAST ASIA PTE. LTD., *Singapore*
WHITEHALL BOOKS LIMITED, *Wellington, New Zealand*

The real purpose of books
is to trap the mind
into doing its own thinking.

—C. Morley

Contents

INTRODUCTION   1

1
FINDING YOUR CORRECT SIZE   3

2
WHAT IS A GOOD FIT?   8

3
HOW TO BEGIN   12

4

PREPARING A SKIRT FOR FIRST FITTING 24

5

FITTING A SKIRT 32

6

BODICE ALTERATIONS 41

7

KNOW YOUR PATTERN 45

8

NECKLINE AND SHOULDER ALTERATIONS 52

9

ARMSCYE AND BUST DART ALTERATIONS 60

10

SLEEVES 65

11

USING YOUR BASIC COMPLETED PATTERN IN GENERAL SEWING 73

12

USING YOUR BASIC PATTERN FOR DESIGNING 77

13

GENERAL SEWING TIPS

93

14

ALTERING FOR THE LARGE WOMAN

103

15

LINE AND DESIGN

110

INDEX

124

Introduction

As I sat pondering over an angle to use in writing this book, it occurred to me that the subject was not angles, but curves and how to make clothes fit them. There are any number of books, for instance, on dieting, or "making your figure fit your clothes." Not every potential dieter, however, can benefit from such a book—perhaps medical reasons or no will power. But I feel that every home sewer or student can benefit from this book; it will show you how to make commercial patterns fit you—all your curves or lack of them. Once you have determined your basic alterations, you can apply them to each commercial pattern you cut as you cut it out. If this sounds like the answer to a lot of your sewing frustrations, it's intended to.

The "perfect fit"—perfection is the goal one strives for. Your degree of perfection may differ from someone else's; it's simply a sense of values. Webster defines *perfect* as "having all the properties naturally belonging to it; complete; sound; flawless." For fit or figure, beauty is in the eye of the beholder. Charles Kleibacker, a Seventh Avenue designer, refers to the "beautiful female anatomy," but I think more along the "bodies are funny" lines—perhaps because I regard my own body as rather funny. But anyone's body—funny or not—can look better. A good fit will flatter your figure by camouflaging what is too narrow, too flat, too broad, or too round, and make those flaws less noticeable. A good fit will give you style and smartness as well as comfort in every garment.

As a clothing construction specialist, I have taught sewing techniques and fitting to thousands of women. In the following chapters I am sure the teacher in me will show through, but I don't want this to read as a sober textbook. I am a strong believer that life without humor is meaningless, and certainly dull.

1 *Finding Your Correct Size*

What size pattern do you wear?

An easy question to answer, you may think. "I wear a size 12 ready-to-wear dress, so I need a size 12 pattern." Not necessarily so. As you probably have realized, in ready-to-wear there is no standardization of sizes. Each designer or manufacturer has his or her own guide for size. For instance, suppose you purchase a designer's dress for $750., and you fit into a marked size 8. That same day you buy a dress at a discount store; you might need a marked size 12! The higher the price you pay, the smaller the size you generally need; the designer is working on your vanity. So when your friend tells you she wears a size 10, and you think she looks bigger, she is probably buying expensive clothes! Remember—ready-to-wear-sizes may not have any relationship to commercial patterns. If you wear a size 12 in ready-to-wear, it does not necessarily mean you wear a size 12 pattern.

Until the early 1950s, pattern sizes sometimes differed according to pattern company, and a size 12 pattern was generally larger than a size 12 in ready-to-wear. With a little urging from the United States government, the major pattern companies got together in the form of the Measurement Standard Committee of the Pattern Industry, and agreed upon a set of body-sizing specifications. In 1967, they revamped the specifications into what many sewers know as "new sizing."

Thus commercial patterns are now standardized, meaning that if you wear a size 12 in one of them, you will buy a size 12 from all companies. The companies under this standardization law are Butterick, Vogue, McCall's and Simplicity. They are the patterns to which the instructions in this book apply. The pattern size charts are based on body measurements. Patterns always include extra inches for body ease. The amount varies with designer and style of garment.

DETERMINING PATTERN SIZE

How do you determine your correct pattern size? There are three ways:

1. Take the measurements the pattern suggests—bust, waist, hip. If your measurements coincide with all three marked on the pattern, that's your size—but you're a rare individual. It could be said that "patterns aren't made for people." The measurements used to set up the standardization for commercial patterns are a mean, an average or cross section of all human body measurements. Patterns with these measurements will come close to fitting all of us, but will truly fit none of us. (And you thought it was just *your* figure!)

2. Since the first method probably will not give your true pattern size, take just the bust measurement, knowing you will have to alter the rest of the pattern. To take your bust measurement correctly, use a tape measure that is true and does not stretch. Hold the tape high under the arms in the back (about where you wear your bra) and across the fullest part of the bust (see Figure 1-1). Take a taut measurement; that is your pattern size (34″ = size 12, 36″ = size 14, 38″ = size 16). The individual with a small bone structure and a large bust needs to take a "high chest measurement". This is done by placing the tape around the body, high in the back and up and over the bustline in front, and adding 2″—that is your pattern size

Figure 1-1. Taking bust measurement

(see Figure 1-2). This method is fairly foolproof, but it does have a couple of flaws. Suppose your bust measurement is 35″— remember that size 12 is 34″, size 14 is 36″. Don't panic. If you do measure 35″, your bra cup size will help you to decide your correct pattern size. If you wear a C cup, purchase the size 12 pattern; if you wear an A cup, buy the size 14 pattern. That sounds backwards until you think about it. The woman with the 35″ A cup is really the bigger person; she gets the measurement across her back. The 35″ C cup woman has it all up front; she has a smaller back and is actually a smaller individual. (Incidentally, all commercial patterns are cut for the B cup bra size.)

3. This is the easiest method of determining pattern size, and it nearly always works. Buy your pattern the same size as you buy your bra. Since this won't work at all if you are buying the wrong bra size, be sure! Bra size is determined by taking your measurement *under* the bust, tautly over the rib cage, holding one finger under the tape

5

Figure 1-2.   Taking high chest measurement

as you measure. If the measurement is less than 33″, add 5″ for bra size; if it is over 33″, add 3″ for bra size. For instance, if your measurement is 31″, your bra size is 36, and your pattern size is 14. If your measurement is 35″, your bra size is 38, and your pattern size is 16. It may not, and probably won't fit everywhere, but it will fit the bust and is your correct pattern size.

Once you have determined correct pattern size, buy all your patterns in that size. Buy by your bra size, determined by Method 3. Most women will have to make hip adjustments in their patterns, which we will discuss later. But buy the size pattern that fits you in the bustline. To alter bust size in a pattern, you probably would need some training in pattern drafting; all other alterations, however, are basically simple. If you buy a size 12 for your 34 bra, buy a size 12 in a skirt or pants or any other pattern. If you are larger in the hip, learn to make the size 12 skirt fit your hips. Why? Suppose you want to buy an expensive designer pattern for a dress? Do you want to

Size	Bust
6	30½
8	31½
10	32½
12	34
14	36
16	38
18	40
20	42

spend money on a size 12 for the bodice and a size 14 for the skirt? If you once learn to make the 12 skirt fit you in a dress pattern, you can buy all standardized patterns in a 12.

So, what size pattern should you buy? "Buy the commercial pattern in the same size as you buy your bra." I might add that there is only a 3/8″ difference between pattern sizes. This is called grading, and it is generally done by computers. So if you use a size 12, but must add "a little" to all side seams, why not buy a 14? This is optional, but I prefer my students to choose a pattern size in the Misses or Women's category, even though there are patterns for Half Sizes and Misses Petites as well. The Half Size and Misses Petite individuals seem to be cheated in choice of patterns. As we know, no pattern is going to fit everywhere, so why not choose a Misses pattern and learn to make *it* fit you—then you have your choice of many designs.

Now that you have determined your correct pattern size, your next step is to find out what a good fit should be. You may be surprised to learn that the right size doesn't insure a good fit.

2 *What Is a Good Fit?*

"If you don't know where you're going, you will end up somewhere else."

—Dr. Lawrence Peter

You have the correct pattern size; now where do you go? To begin with, every garment should be in perfect balance and proportion in relation to the individual figure. It should fit smoothly and should never have to be pulled into place. We have all seen the woman who has to tug her skirt down and into place when she stands up. The skirt is simply too tight. Each garment hangs by its own weight, from the shoulders for the bodice and from the waistline for the skirt. A good fit gives an illusion of perfection. As for the amount of ease that is the most flattering, here is a good guide: 4″ of ease in the bustline (a 1 ″ pinch of fabric in the front and a 1 ″ pinch in back) the waistline must fit to perfection, no ease; the hips need at least 2 ″ of ease (a ½ ″ pinch of fabric in front and a ½ ″ pinch in back). This guide is adaptable for a closely fitted garment. As you know, the style of a garment determines the true amount of ease. For instance, 4″ of ease in the bustline of a strapless dress would be a disaster!

KEY POINTS FOR GOOD FIT

To determine a good fit, let's start at the top. The shoulder seam should fall on top of the natural shoulder *and 1″* behind the ear lobe, as you look straight ahead. Since you can't check that on yourself, find a "so and sew buddy". The neckline should be smooth at the base of the neck, no draglines or pulling. Shoulder width is determined by the bone that joins your arm to your shoulder; where they join you set in the sleeve.

Let's consider the bustline; if you wear a B cup bra size, you have far less problems than the A's, C's, and others. As we said before, patterns are cut for the B cup bra, recutting is necessary if you don't fit the cup. The bust dart, as well as waistline darts, should point to the crest of the bust, but darts should stop short of the fullness. The amount they "stop short of" is determined by the shape of the bust.

The waist seam falls on your natural waistline, the smallest part of your midsection. It is often difficult to determine an exact location, particularly if you grew up during the shift dress silhouette. To locate your exact waistline, tie a piece of rayon hem tape around your midsection—where it sits comfortably is your waistline. No ease in this area, but not too tight either. Remember—well-fitted clothes are comfortable, not *too* roomy.

Sleeves should be comfortable and well fitted once the bodice shoulder and armsyce (shape of the armhole) have been altered correctly. Fold your arm to your waist; elbow darts point to the bend of the elbow and the finished length stops at the point where the hand ends and the wrist begins.

Skirts seem to give less fitting problems than a bodice; the side seam on a skirt must hang—plumb—from the underarm, or perpendicular to the floor. When the side seam swings to the back, it makes the skirt shorter in the back. When the side seam swings to the front, it makes the skirt shorter in front. Skirt darts are fitted by pointing the front darts to the hipbone. Back skirt darts are determined by the shape of the derrière. Darts will differ in number, according to shape of hip and derrière. The length of the dart? Darts stop short of fullness; if a bubble occurs at the end of the dart, shorten the dart.

9   (That is probably the opposite of what you usually have done.)

To fit successfully, you must observe the figure keenly and study the relationships among its contours, just as a sculptor would. You must become conscious of fabric grain to know where and when to adjust it. And you must learn to trace wrinkles and unwanted bulges to their origin before you can correct them.

Figure 2-1.   There is a relationship between sewer and sculptor

These are a few guidelines to help you determine whether you need to read on—if your clothes reach all these standards, you need not read further. Of course, you may not only sew for yourself, so. . . .

11

One's own figure and taste should be the basis for selection of pattern style and cut of garment. How many times have you made a poor pattern selection for your figure type? Once you have learned your alterations, you should choose patterns that make such alterations as easy as possible.

3 How to Begin

Before beginning any sewing project, you should understand the grain of the fabric and its relationship to your figure and a good fit. The key grain lines or balance lines on your body are shown in Figure 3-1.

The crosswise grain lines must be parallel to the floor, and the lengthwise grain lines perpendicular to them. A discrepancy in these grain lines indicates an alteration. Although we will be referring to "alterations" throughout the book, what we will be doing at the end of it is "cutting to fit." What is the difference? An alteration is a correction made on a garment that already has been constructed, such as a fitting dress or shell. You must see "cloth on a body" before you can determine any alterations. Measurements mean very little; they are a guide, but they cannot determine an actual alteration. If you haven't already learned—the tape measure does lie. We will do very little measuring to determine alterations.

Cutting to fit means that you make the "learned" alterations on

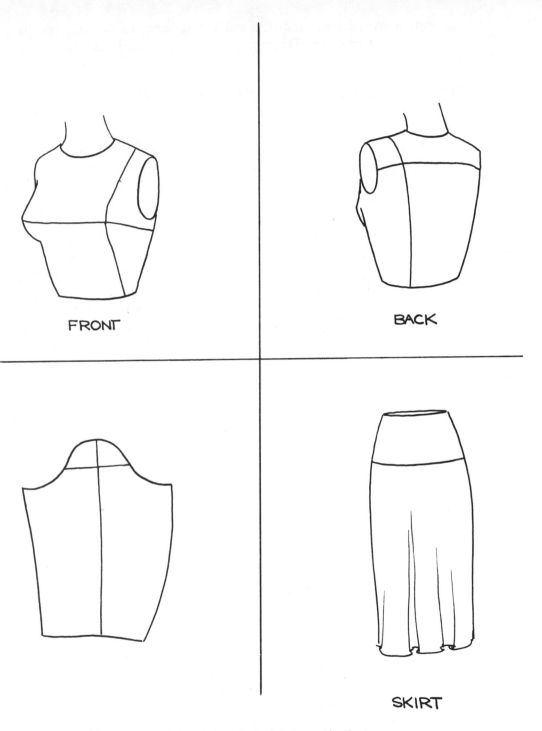

FRONT

BACK

SKIRT

13   **Figure 3-1.**   **The body's key grain lines**

the tissue pattern, and then cut the garment to fit your specifications. No ripping and fitting—just cut, stitch, and wear.

TAKING PERSONAL MEASUREMENTS FOR A SKIRT

Get out your tape measure. But remember that the following measurements are only a guide for your personal pattern.

It is possible to alter a skirt and get a fair fit the first time by taking your measurements and comparing them to the basic tissue pattern. You are beginning to "cut to fit."

Since we know it is necessary to see cloth on a body, a basic fitting dress is suggested. Each pattern company has one available. Pinning the tissue pattern together and trying it on is of little or no value; only fabric will tell the true story. Making the fitted dress (often called a shell) with a waistline will help you to understand better *all* your personal fitting needs. Your alterations are then suitable to determine pattern adjustments for all styles. (Make a fitting dress in firm, but not stiff, fabric. It should be soft enough to contour to the body and strong enough to be ripped apart—altered—without distorting the grain. A cotton/polyester blend is good. Do not use unbleached muslin or an old sheet; neither contour to the body nor drape as any other fabric. Also, do not use a knit for this fitting dress; we will be fitting by the grain, which is nonexistent in knits.)

Fitting is done with the garment right side out, and it should be done only on one side. All changes should be transferred to the other half of the garment after a fitting.

Before starting on Step 1, turn to the chart at the back of the book to record your measurements.

Step 1. Waist Measurement

Measure the waistband of a skirt (or pants) that fits you comfortably all day. Your waistline may vary as much as 2″ during a day. Have you ever measured your waistline and found the exact same measurement? Not likely! List the waistband measurement on the chart. I often call this a "compromise" measurement, as we are compromising between the tiny waist before breakfast and the fuller waist after dinner and dessert.

14

Step 2. Hip Measurement

Take an "as you would like to wear it" measurement at the largest part of your hip (Figure 3-2). Books used to advise measureing at 7″ below the waist. Today the average is 8″, but you can be largest at 3″ or 12″ below the waist, or any place in between. Look in the mirror again, and see where *you* are largest in the hip. "As you would like to wear it" means exactly that—how you personally want your skirt to hug or not to hug the hips. Less than 2″ of ease is undesirable, however, even for a stand-up cocktail party dress, and certainly you need lots more ease if that skirt is going bowling. The decision is your personal choice, but do take into consideration your age and figure type. If you're 18 years old, tall, and willowy, fit the skirt with little ease, but if you are 21 plus and a somewhat spreading willow, give the "as you would like to wear it" measurement a little more ease. Put this measurement on the chart.

Step 3. Skirt Length—Personal (Figure 3-3)

Determine your skirt length by taking this measurement as shown in Figure 3-3. Measure on the halfway mark of your body. Don't ever determine length measurements at center front or center back. The halfway mark is one-half the way from center front to side seam, and measure only on the front of the skirt. Let the 1″ end of the tape measure drop to the finished edge of the skirt (it is easiest to wear a skirt whose length you like) and nip the tape in at your waistline; that is the finished length of your skirt. Add 2½″ for normal turn of hem, and that is your cutting length. This measurement is added to the chart.

FLAT MEASURING THE SKIRT PATTERN

Now we must "flat measure" the tissue pattern to determine pattern measurement. To flat measure a pattern means to measure the tissue pattern as it is flat on a table. Do not include seam allowances as you flat measure.

16   **Figure 3-2.   Measuring the hips**

Figure 3-3.   Finding skirt length

Step 1.

Do not flat measure the waistline of any skirt pattern. Read the waist measurement on your pattern envelope and believe what it says (at least temporarily). Jot down this figure on the chart under pattern measurement.

Step 2.

Flat measure the hip area of the pattern at the largest part of your hip; if you are largest at 8″, measure that area. Do not include seam allowances when you flat measure a tissue pattern; you did not include seam allowances when you measured your body. Record your findings.

Step 3.

To check length of skirt measure at the halfway mark on the front of the skirt only, make a mark on the tissue. From this mark you will add or subtract an equal amount to the bottom of both front and back of the skirt. Do not split the pattern where indicated, but add or subtract to the bottom edge. By altering an A-line skirt where the tissue indicates, you are cutting a slice out of the middle of a bell and trying to put it back together. Don't! Add or subtract to the bottom cut edge (see Figure 3-4). Make this alteration on your tissue pattern. There is no reason actually to list it on your chart, as every skirt length will measure differently. You always will need to flat measure skirt tissues in hip area and length. Each pattern company and designer varies the amount of ease; fashion and personal choice vary the length. From the measurement chart you should be able to compare your personal measurement with the pattern measurement, and determine plus or minus to your own pattern.

You will note that we are fitting and altering only one side of figure and pattern. (In commercial patterns, generally only the right half is given.) When you looked in the mirror, you may have noticed that you are not perfectly symmetrical. The right side and the left side of your face are not the same, nor are the right and left sides of your body. How many of us have a high shoulder or a high hip? It is easiest to cut for the largest side, and cut off or alter the smaller side. If the discrepancy is great, you will have to cut for both sides separately.

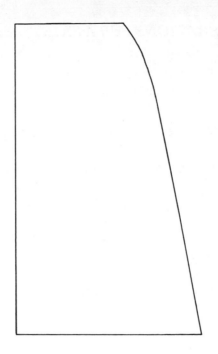

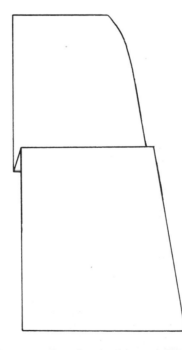

Figure 3-4. (Top) Correct way to lengthen or shorten A-line skirt; (Bottom) Incorrect way

19

To make your corrections (plus or minus), you will need the following alterations:

Alteration 1. Increasing Hip (Figure 3-5)

If your measurement indicates an additional amount necessary in the hip area, add an equal amount from top to bottom on the side seam only. Never add to center front or center back. Let us say, for instance, that you need 4″ of additional fabric for the hip area. You will add 1″ to the side seam of the skirt front. Make the same addition to the back side seam. Each of these is cut on the double, so you are actually adding 4″. (Yes, you have enlarged the waistline; *just keep that in mind.*) Maintain a straight line by adding equally as shown.

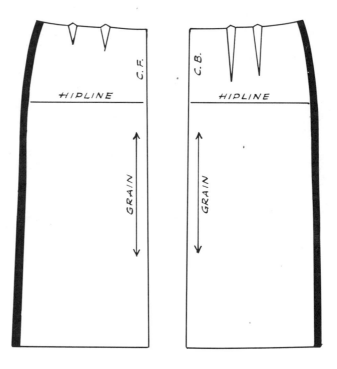

Figure 3-5.   Increasing hip

Alteration 2. Decreasing Hip (Figure 3-6)

If you need to subtract from the hipline, it is done in the same way. Simply subtract ¼th of the total amount from the side seam. (If you need to remove more than 4 times 5/8″ seam, or 2½″, you must do so by taking a fold on the halfway mark of your skirt pattern. Note that a ¼″ fold removes ½″ of tissue. Cut on the double; that removes 1″ from the front and 1″ from the back. This alteration is rarely needed, since the individual would be two sizes larger in the bust than the hips!)

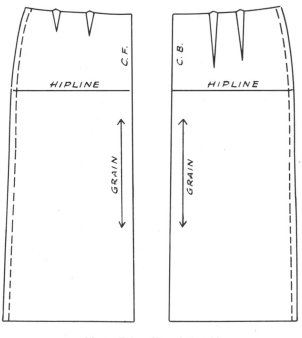

Figure 3-6.   Decreasing hip

Alteration 3. Increasing Waistline (Figure 3-7)

You already may have made the necessary corrections to the waist when you made the hipline alteration. (Hip alterations are always done first. Make each alteration separate and complete before going on to the next.) Or you may now need an additional waistline alteration because of the hipline alteration you have already done.

21

To add to the waistline of a skirt, add the amount (¼ of the total) to the waist and taper to nothing at the largest part of your hip. Again, do the same alteration to front and back. You are cutting on the double, so 1″ on front and back waist would give you a total of 4″ in the waistline.

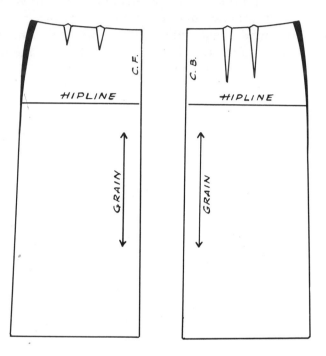

Figure 3-7.   Increasing waistline

Alteration 4. Decreasing Waistline (Figure 3-8)

If you have dieted away those extra inches and your waistline is smaller than the pattern, you may increase the darts, but the maximum increase to each dart is 1/8″. (You are stitching 1/8″ on the double, removing ¼″ of fabric—and ¼″ times the number of darts in the skirt equals the amount removed.) Any additional subtraction would have to be done as you see "cloth on a body," your first fitting. Do not remove from the side seam until you have seen the skirt on your figure.

These four alterations are made on the tissue pattern before you cut out the skirt. Always remember that your tissue pattern is like a blueprint; you must make any correction or addition to it before cutting or stitching. Like any construction work, alterations, or any pattern work, must be done with precision. Your paper work is very important to the finished constructed garment. The end result will show the amount of care and effort you put into it.

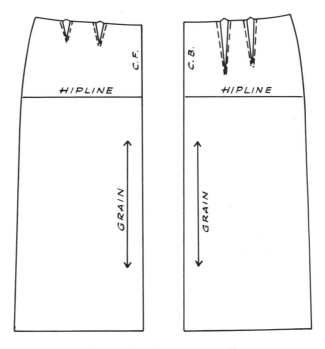

Figure 3-8.   Decreasing waistline

4 *Preparing a Skirt For First Fitting*

Construction is extremely important when you are learning basic alterations. I tell my students over and over again, I can fit them only as well as they stitch. Accuracy in stitching a 5/8″ seam is of absolute necessity, or you may determine the incorrect alteration. Blocking, straightening, or relaxing your fabric is even more important.

MAKING FABRIC GRAIN PERFECT

If your garment is not cut grain perfect (distorted or twisted on the body as shown in Figure 4-1), it will hang "off grain," and you will learn the incorrect alterations. All fabrics are woven grain perfect with lengthwise (warp) and crosswise (woof) threads at right angles to each other. Fabric is temporarily pulled "off grain" in manufacturing, either by the finishing process or folding and bolting. You must block every piece of fabric before cutting.

Figure 4-1.   An "off grain" dress

First, tear the fabric on the crosswise grain from selvage to selvage on both ends. If the fabric will not tear, pull a thread or two and cut on rippled threads (Figure 4-2). Fold the fabric lengthwise, and the

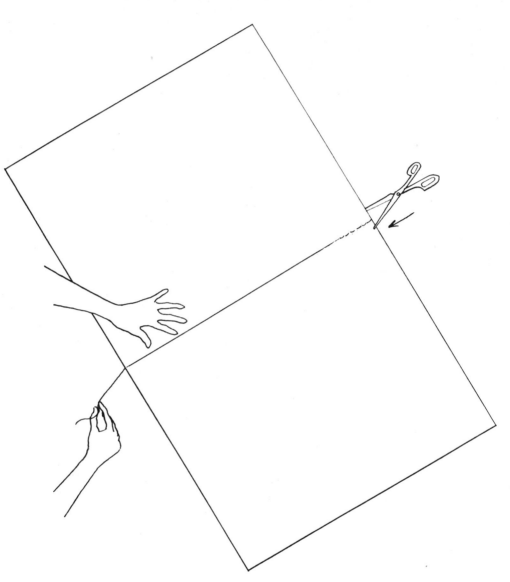

Figure 4-2. Straightening the fabric

crosswise ends should match and be at right angles to the lengthwise. (Check this right angle with the edge of your cutting table or a book.)

Many of today's fabrics have a resin finish on them, so they require little or no ironing. (If you use the cotton/polyester blend, the no-ironing characteristic comes from the blend.) The resin needs to be softened by the heat and steam of an iron. With the fabric folded, press along the lengthwise grain (do not iron, use an up and down pressing motion). Work from selvage to fold, touching every inch of fabric, heating the resin and relaxing the grain. Whenever possible, small lengths of fabric should be blocked, for example, the skirt length in one piece and the bodice length in another (Figure 4-3).

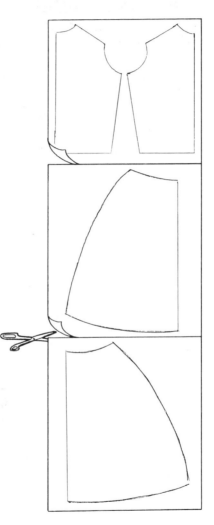

Figure 4-3.   **Cutting lengths**

When the fabric is ready for cutting, it should be flat on the table with the crosswise edges at right angles to the lengthwise edges. The fabric is relaxed, and this allows *YOU* to relax as you cut and stitch. (Beware of bonded fabrics, permanent press, chintz, and highly polished cottons. Their threads or grain are permanently held in position. This causes the grain of the fabric to hang distorted on your figure. It can never be relaxed or made to fit properly.)

SKIRT CONSTRUCTION

Once the skirt is cut grain perfect with your cutting to fit alterations, you are ready for construction. Directionally stay stitch the skirt ½ " from edges in required areas (Figure 4-4). Stitch side seams from bottom to top, 5/8". Do not insert a zipper in the fitting shell. Leave an opening at the center back since fewer alterations are done in that area. In stitching a fitting garment together, machine baste in contrasting thread those seams where alterations are expected so that they may be ripped apart easily.

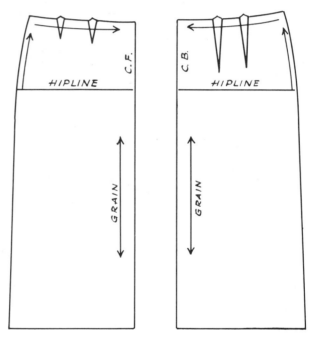

Figure 4-4.   Directional stay stitching

You may wish to stitch the darts indicated on the pattern. You *could* be the individual the pattern was made for, but the chances aren't too good. I prefer just to tuck or make trouser pleats where the darts are marked.

28

Now you are ready for a process that may be new to many of you. It is called "taping," and it is the kindest thing you can do for your figure.

Taping A Skirt With A Center Back Closure

Use rayon seam tape for this procedure. It is not necessary to preshrink the tape before using. It *will* shrink, but since everyone tends to tape the waistline too loose, the shrinkage will make it fit just right.

A few facts to note: Your waistline is the smallest part of your midsection; above and below you are larger (at least, most women are!) You are larger across the front than the back. If you have a 24″ waist, you are *not* 12″ across the front and 12″ across the back. But you *are* 12″ from center front to center back on the right side, as you are 12″ from center front to center back on the left side. So keep in mind, as you complete the following taping steps, that you are not quartering your waistline; you *are* larger across the front.

1. Pin the center point of tape on the inside of the skirt at the center front (see Figure 4-5).

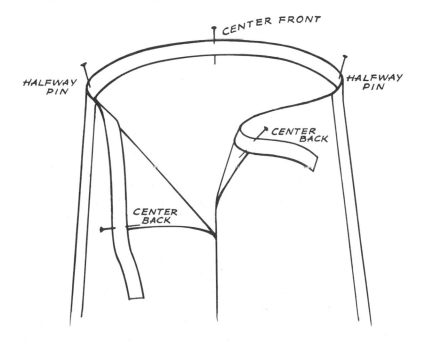

Figure 4-5.   Taping the waistline

2. From this pin, measure along the tape for ½ of your waist measurement, and mark with a pin this point on the tape.

3. Match this point with center back of the skirt (½ of your waist measurement from center front to center back).

4. Hold skirt up by the center front and center back pins.

5. Check the "drop" at the side seam. The average drop is approximately 1½ ", but who is average? If your "drop" is slight, you have a telephone pole figure; waist and hip are close to the same measurement. If your "drop" is great, you are the hourglass figure; tiny waist with rounded hips. You probably fall between these two extremes. After checking the drop, if the skirt is smaller than the tape, decrease tucks or darts.

6. Fold tape in half from center front to center back, and place a pin at this point (halfway of tape).

7. Fold skirt in half from center front to center back, and place a pin halfway of skirt. This should fall on the *front* of the skirt, not on the side seam.

8. Match the two halfway pins together, but place a third pin in the tape at the side seam, where the tape falls. (Remove the two pins placed in steps 6 and 7.)

9. The other half of the skirt should be the same measurement from center front to side seam and center back to side seam as obtained in step 8.

10. Check to see that the ease on both sides of the skirt front and the skirt back are the same (equal amount of ease in all four sections).

Stitch the tape to the inside of the skirt, attaching the lower edge of the tape on the 5/8 " seam allowance of the skirt. Stitch with the skirt on the bed of the sewing machine, tape up. Increase the pressure (*not* the tension) on your machine; that will help you to ease the skirt to the tape without gathers.

If you are not familiar with the pressure gauge on your machine, refer to your sewing machine instruction book. Each machine is different; some have an automatic pressure gauge and almost do just what you tell them! The pressure gauge also is used for varying weights of fabric. Release the pressure for a heavy wool or double knit (to let it under the foot), and increase the pressure for a sheer or lightweight fabric (to hold it in place). Note: Your sewing machine instruction book may tell you the opposite; one well-known brand does just that.

To help you remember—it is right to tighten and left to loosen, whether it be tension, pressure, or the lid on a catsup bottle. To increase the pressure for taping, turn the dial to the right.

Once you have completed the taping process and find that the skirt waistline fits you correctly, you may use these same measurements to tape every skirt you make (see Figure 4-6). For instance, if you measure 6½″ from center front to side seam and 6″ from center back to side seam, use these measurements on every tape. It is suggested that you tape every skirt, dress, and pair of pants you make from now on. That is custom fitting, for your waistline and yours alone.

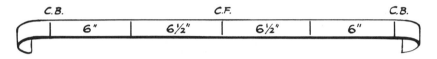

Figure 4-6. Marked tape

5 *Fitting a Skirt*

Now your skirt is ready for the first fitting. Since you cannot truly fit yourself accurately, enlist a "sew buddy," someone you don't mind letting know what your figure is really like!

Before you try on any fitting garment, you should consider your underclothing. There was a time when it would have been understood that you would wear a bra and girdle for a fitting. But times have changed! Do wear a good bra and a control garment in the hip area. Even though many girls and women say they "never wear a girdle," for fitting purposes some type of support really is necessary. Even panty hose with support tops will do. The same darts that are fitted on you while wearing the support garment will fit you at all times. (Caution: Never wear bikini pants and panty hose for a fitting; that will give you two waistlines. Also be sure that panty hose elastic is right at your waist when fitting.)

Figure 5-1.   "Sew buddies"

1. Even though we have said that you could allow the amount of ease you personally wear in the skirt, try this test. With the skirt on, take hold of it at the hipline and lift it 6″; it should drop back by it's own weight. If you have to wiggle it back in place, it's too tight. You should have added more to the side seams in cutting.

2. Be sure that the waist tape fits you correctly, no ease. If it is not secure, you may cause yourself a unneeded alteration. Now check to see if you are "plumb" (the dictionary defines plumb as "a lead weight attached to a line and used to indicate a vertical direction; straight down or up: vertically"). The side seams as well as the center back seam of your skirt should fall perpendicular to the floor. Make a plumb bob with a weight hanging on the end of a piece of rayon seam tape. If your center back seam is not plumb, you have a high hip. If the side seam swings to the front, you have a flat derriere; if the side seam swings to the back, you have a protruding derriere. (That shelf in the back also could be caused by the new girdle you just purchased to flatten your tummy. It did, but the inches had to go someplace. Girdles don't make you smaller, they just redistribute the flesh!) See Figure 5-2 for body types.

3. Correct the plumb line as follows:

High Hip

(As a note of interest, most of us are not born with a high hip. It is usually caused by carrying books, groceries, or a heavy baby. The high hip an individual is born with is usually due to a curvature of the spine, giving the person one high shoulder as well. Today's living may give us less high hips—we don't carry things around as much—but it *is* giving us more high shoulders, due to the popularity of shoulder bags. Seems funny, but our way of life and fashion can change our figures.) Add the amount the center back seam swings off to the high hip at the waistline, tapering to nothing at center back (Figure 5-3). This will automatically straighten (or plumb) the center back seam and straighten the hem. Note: The higher hip could be rounder or larger as well, so the same darts may not do for both hips.

Figure 5-2. Body types (l. to r.): high hip, protruding derriere, flat derriere, the "plumb woman"

Flat Derriere

When the side seam swings to the front, decrease the center back at the waistline by this amount, as shown (Figure 5-4), tapering to nothing at the side seam.

Protruding Derriere

If the side seam swings to the back, decrease the center front at the waistline by this amount, tapering to nothing at the side seam (Figure 5-5).

Now you're plumb, as is the young lady in Figure 5-6! (Note: You have not only straightened the plumb line, but you have straightened or corrected the hem as well. Be sure you are making these cuttings to fit alterations to your pattern as you go.)

35

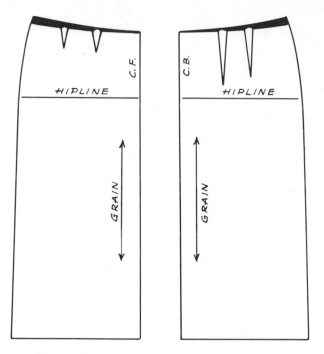

Figure 5-3. Correcting the high hip plumb line

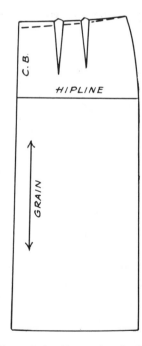

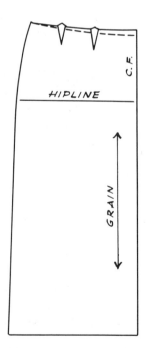

**Figure 5-4. Correcting the flat
derriere plumb line**

**Figure 5-5. Correcting the protruding
derriere plumb line**

Figure 5-6.   Miss "Plumb Perfect"

4. Now that you have the skirt hanging straight of grain on your body, consider the darts. The darts on the front of a skirt must point to the hipbone. In a true "basic pattern" for designing purposes, the center line of the darts should be straight of grain, but for the home sewer a slightly slanted dart often is more flattering. The number of darts across the front of your skirt is determined by your curve (the amount of padding over the hipbone). The barrel figure may look best with no darts, just an equal amount of ease across the tummy. The barrel figure rounds quickly from the waist and leaves just a little ease, not enough fabric for a dart construction. Other figure types will have to try darts on their fitting partners, you may require one dart, two, or possibly three. The number of darts has nothing to do with the size of the individual. For instance, three very small darts would cause the fabric to protrude less than one large dart. For darts in the back or derriere, the learnings are the same. Usually an individual gets two back darts, and the one closer to center back is longer than the other one—but not *always*. Again, the barrel figure would have no darts, and other figures would get one to three. Gently shape the darts over the curve, don't force them. Your first inclination is usually right. Don't try too hard.

5. Once you think you have determined the location, the stitching of the darts becomes very important. If you are flat, stitch a straight dart, but if you curve below the waistline, try an inside curved dart as shown (Figure 5-7). Many figures require straight darts in the back and inside curved darts on the front. Does your own figure curve out quickly from the waist?

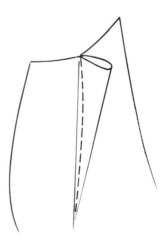

Figure 5-7. Inside curved dart

6. Terminate or end darts quickly, securing or knotting them one thread from the fold of the fabric. Always stitch from the wide end to the point of the dart. After you have stitched the darts, try the skirt on again. If they dimple at the bottom, *shorten them*. You've always lengthened them, haven't you? That simply pushed the dimple farther down; the dart terminates *above* the fullness to shape the fabric over the fullness.

After following these steps, you should have a pretty good fit, at least better than you started with. There are, however, a few other alterations for an even better fit:

1. A minor thing to correct is the skirt that hikes up at center front, just a little. Just add a bit (½ inch or less) to the center front of your skirt and taper to nothing at the side seams. You are cutting the skirt straighter of grain at the top. Some "big tummys" may need to add more than straight of grain at center front (Figure 5-8)—or buy a better girdle.

2. If your front darts are giving you too much shape over the hip-bone, you may decrease the waist as shown in Figure 5-9. But never more than 5/8", you'll be distorting the grain too much.

3. Something still wrong? Get out the plumb bob and drop it from your underarm. If one side seam is plumb, does it cut the body in

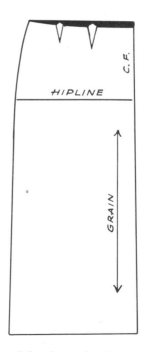

Figure 5-8. Increasing the tummy

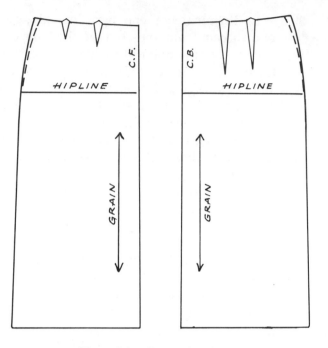

Figure 5-9.   Decreasing the waist

half? (Hip area only, ignore your legs right now.) You may need a larger skirt in the front than in the back, or vice versa. So adding an equal amount to front and back will not always hold true when you see "cloth on a body." Relocate the side seam by decreasing one side seam and increasing the other. On the tissue pattern first!

The skirt is actually easy to alter and fit. Since it is supported only by the waist tape, the entire area below the hips swings free. So the slightest flaw in balance of grain is obvious by the way the skirt hangs.

6 *Bodice Alterations*

The bodice of a dress generally gives one a bit more difficulty with fitting than the skirt. If you keep one thing in mind before you begin, you'll find the going much easier. Remember that *commercial patterns are cut for the B cup bra.* Those of you who are an A cup, C cup, or larger must make an alteration to the tissue pattern before you can cut your fitting dress. Bust darts will not be the same size in various cups. The larger the size of dart stitched, the greater the bulge it produces.

To get the "feel" for fitting darts, you may want to do some experimenting in the kitchen (see Figure 6-1). You will need a paper towel to fit over various objects, such as a grapefruit, orange, egg. You'll see that the grapefruit takes a larger dart than the orange, and the fried egg doesn't get much of a dart at all. Which category do you fit into?

Figure 6-1. Practice fitting

A Cup Alterations

If you are in the "egg" category, instead of altering, you may prefer purchasing a padded bra—your clothes will hang better. If you are not one for pretense, however, you can make an alteration. Decrease the size of the dart and shorten the front length of the bodice by the same amount (Figure 6-2).

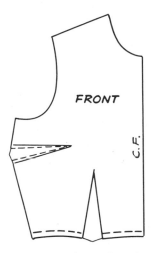

Figure 6-2. A cup alterations

C Cup and Larger Alterations

Throughout this book, I will seldom ask you to slash a pattern. It is best and easiest to increase or decrease the outside edge of your pattern; the less distortion from the original pattern, the better. But, in the case of C cup and larger alterations, you can achieve with one slash what would ordinarily be three or four steps. I can only suggest what you need to do this alteration, as everyone may require a different amount. (For the C cup, I suggest 5/8"; beyond that, you will probably need to see "cloth on a body.")

1. Continue drawing the center lines of the darts until they cross on your pattern. Where they cross is the crest of the bust (B in Figure 6-3).
2. Slash on the center line of the bust dart (only) to the point of crossing (A to B).
3. Make your own slash, halfway of the shoulder and slash to the point of crossing (C to B).

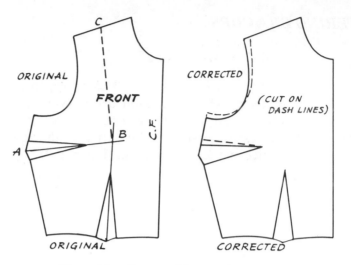

Figure 6-3. C cup, and larger, alterations

4. Overlap slash C = B by 5/8″. You will be shortening the shoulder length by 5/8″. That automatically narrows the shoulder, raises the underarm, and enlarges the bust dart. The increased dart you needed and the raised underarm eliminates that wrinkle or dragline from armscye to bust. Most of you require the narrower shoulder as well. (We will discuss increasing or decreasing shoulder width later.) Buying patterns by bust measurement should give the correct circumference for the armscye to fit comfortably. If it still gaps in front, you may need to add something (¼″) to the front underarm seam. Add the same amount to the sleeve front underarm seam (see Figure 6-4).

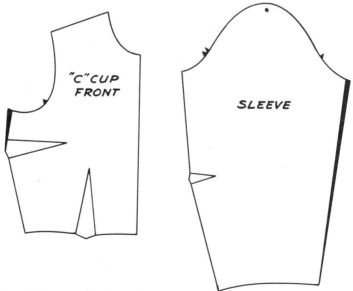

Figure 6-4. Correction for gaping armscye

7 *Know Your Pattern*

"Know thyself," but for the perfect fit, you must know your pattern as well, so you can compare them.

Pattern companies, like others, attempt to cater to the whims of the public. One example is in the production of 45″ piece fabric. The American woman demanded 45″ fabric because she thought she was getting more for her money. There is a long strip left over in 45″ fabric; you don't need it but it *seems* like you are getting more. However, Europeans wouldn't convert their looms from 36″ or 60″ because most designers purchase only 36″ or 60″ fabric due to the waste in 45″ goods. The 36″ fabric allows you to purchase by lengths—front length, plus back length, plus sleeve length, plus details such as the collar.

ALTERING COMMERCIAL PATTERNS

Let's study the pattern. If you compare front and back bodice armscye (armhole) lengths, you will find that the back is longer than the front. You actually have only one armscye length (as

45

one crotch length; note the similarities in the shape of armscye seam and crotch seam). Why not try folding out the extra length in the back scye? Fold it out about halfway down the armscye. You later may need to add a little on to square the shoulder, or to give greater width to the underarm ("Reaching Room"). You end up with a shorter but wider armscye (see Figure 7-1).

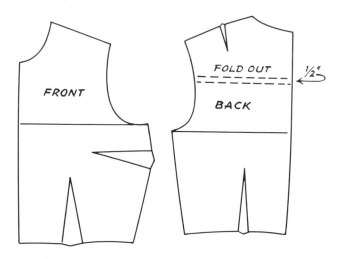

Figure 7-1. Shortening armscye

This alteration may be only for the brave or experienced sewer, but give it some thought. In European-cut garments, the armscye is cut high and close to the body, giving the individual a taller and slimmer appearance. (And many of us would like to look taller and slimmer.) The higher armscye gives you more freedom. You can lift your arm easier and not have the bodice pull up. Our great-grandmothers wore fitted bodices, high armscyes, high necklines, and long sleeves. They did churning, canning, and all kinds of hard work with no ripped clothes. Today's woman generally wants loose-fitting garments in which to work. But, believe it or not, a closer fit really is more comfortable.

When pattern companies brought out new sizing in 1967, they gave a narrower back to the bodice. I find that 95 per cent of my students need more back width. Here's how you get it: To add total back width, trace the neck edge as it is, and turn corner to A (Figure 7-2). Then slide the pattern over 3/8" (one pattern size) and trace the rest of the pattern. You made no change to the outline of the bodice with the exception of lengthening the back shoulder seam. Many people will need more than 3/8″ total width. The average back needs 3/8″ (one pattern size); the narrow individual may wish to cut the pattern as it is.

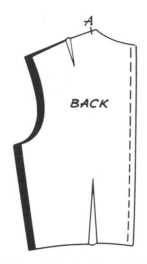

Figure 7-2.   **Total back width**

It is necessary for you to determine bodice length tentatively before cutting—"tentatively" because the tape measure will lie to you and you will need to make slight adjustments later. Take your bodice length measurement on the halfway mark of your body. Add ½″ (for breathing) to that. For the front, this is taken from the halfway point of the shoulder seam over the fullest part of the bust and nipped in at your waist measurement; then add the ½″. Note this measurement on the chart in the back of the book. Take the back bodice measurement from the shoulder seam over the shoulder blade and nipped in at the waistline; add ½″ (Figure 7-3). Record on the chart. Then flat measure the tissue pattern length on the halfway mark, not including seam allowances. You will learn whether it is necessary to lengthen or shorten the bodice of this pattern. Record on the chart.

If you are the All-American girl with a lot up front, you also undoubtedly add front bodice length (Figure 7-4) and nothing to the back as shown (Figure 7-5). This causes the front side seam to be longer than the back. Increase the front bust dart by the amount you added to the front length. You need a larger dart anyway. Or the flat chested (Figure 7-6) may need to add to back length only. This causes the back side seam to be longer than the front, so you

Figure 7-3.   Measuring bodice length

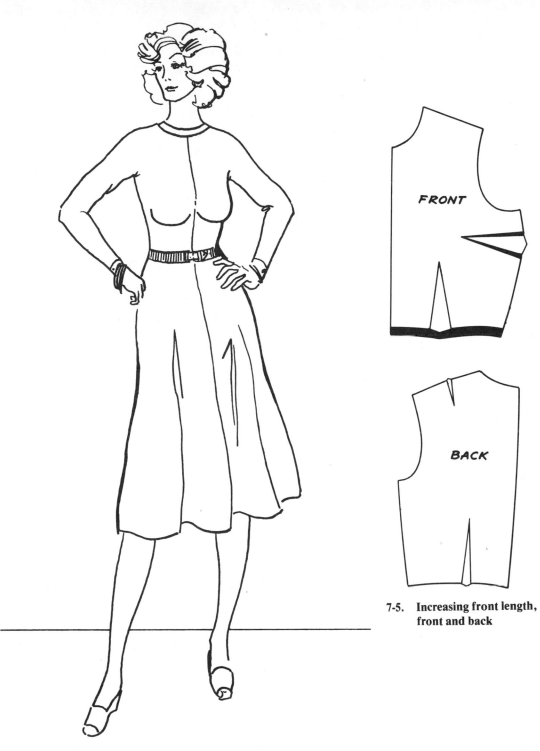

FRONT

BACK

7-5. Increasing front length, front and back

Figure 7-4   All-American Girl

49

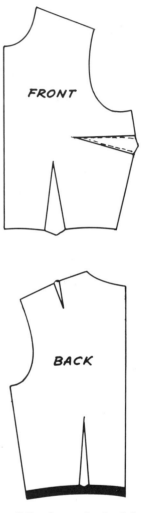

Figure 7-7. Increasing back length

Figure 7-6.

decrease the bust dart by the amount you increased the back length (Figure 7-7).

To put it more simply, decrease or increase bodice length as needed and fold out the bust dart until the side seams match. You could have been decreasing bodice length instead of increasing bodice length, and you would solve the side seam problem the same way.

Note that we increase or decrease bodice length at the bottom edge; do not fold or add where it says "increase or decrease bodice length here." You get the same results either way, but you haven't cut up your pattern.

Until now you may have noted that the skirt and bodice alterations have no relation to each other. And rightly so, as many of us are a different size up than down. But in a fitting dress, you must get the two together—attaching bodice to skirt. So, if you increase the waistline of the skirt, you will add the same amount to the waistline of the bodice, as in Figure 7-8. (Remember, you do not flat measure

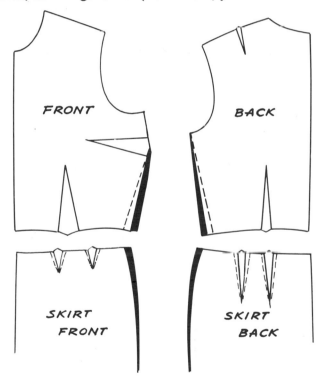

Figure 7-8. Waistline alteration

the pattern at the waistline.) If you decrease the waist of the skirt, you will decrease the waist of the bodice. (As on the skirt, this extra is often needed for ease. You may wish to leave it for a try on).

8 *Neckline and Shoulder Alterations*

Don't expect miracles! Even though you already have made a few alterations, you probably don't look that great—yet. Just keep telling yourself, "This takes time, but each fitting is better than the one I had before."

To touch once more on construction, you should always directionally stay stitch a bodice. If not, it will not "stay" as originally cut. Stay stitch ½ " from the edge directionally, as in Figure 8-1. (Sleeves are *always* stitched into armscye for a fitting. Setting in sleeves will be discussed in Chapter 10.)

NECKLINE FIT

The neckline should lay flat and fit comfortably, not as in Figure 8-2. If you get draglines or folds, the following alteration is necessary.

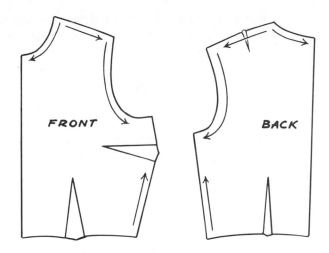

Figure 8-1. Directional stay stitching on bodice

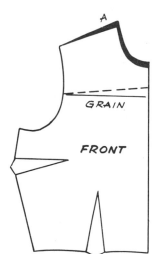

53   Figure 8-2.

Figure 8-3. Adding to neck edge

Raise the neck edge and redraw, but do not change the shape or size of the neckline. Draw around corner to A (Figure 8-3). This insures the original neckline. True up the normal shoulder line. Note that the dotted line was the grain in the original. The solid line is the grain line after the alteration. We have straightened the grain, as well as eliminated the draglines. You also need this alteration if you find it uncomfortable to button the top button of a shirt, or if high neck lines are too tight for you. No, you don't just cut them out; you're not ready for designing yet!

The same neckline alteration may be done to the back of the bodice as well, but in that case it is called a "dowager curve." The dictionary says a dowager is a "widow holding property or a title received from her deceased husband" or an "elderly woman of *imposing* appearance," as in Figure 8-4. Whoever named this altera-

Figure 8-4.

tion was obviously trying to flatter someone; it is needed to compensate for rounded back! That includes many of us—bridge player, the seamstress, car pool driver, student (Figure 8-5). We live in a "Round Shoulder World." So it is possible that you will need the alteration both front and back, by the same amount or by different amounts (Figure 8-6).

If the grain lines across the armscye section of your bodice have not been straightened yet, you may need the square shoulder alteration. (Figure 8-7) It is done in this way:

Figure 8-5.   Wearing the dowager curve

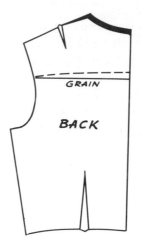

Figure 8-6.   Alteration for the dowager curve

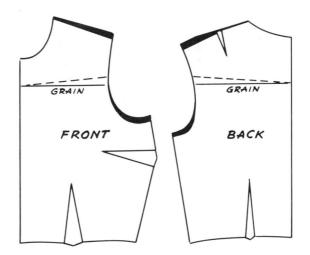

Figure 8-7.   Square shoulder alteration

Using your pattern as a guide, raise the armscye as shown, tracing the identical armscye again, merely relocated. The additional length to underarm or side seam probably will be removed from the bodice length, but your body may use it up. This square shoulder alteration 56 may be done to front or back, and sometimes to both.

Now let's locate where the sleeves should be set in, or actually the shoulder width. Pivot your arm back and forth; feel that bone on the front shoulder move. That's where the arm is set in; that's where you set the sleeve in.

If a garment is too wide on the shoulder, it will feel too tight or binding. So when it feels tight, make it *smaller*. To decrease the shoulder width, use your pattern and retrace the same armscye, but use the notches at A (Figure 8-8) as a pivot. You are decreasing the amount needed at the shoulder, and you taper to nothing at the notches. To increase the shoulder width, pivot at the notches, extending

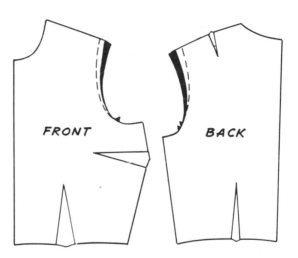

Figure 8-8. Shoulder width

the shoulder as needed. Maintain that same armscye; you will have to set that same sleeve into it.

Decreasing and increasing the shoulder width may be done to both front and back, but seldom by the same amount. In fact, many of you may need to increase the back shoulder width and decrease the front shoulder width.

Check your corrected shoulder seams front and back pattern (Figure 8-9). You *should* end up with the back shoulder seam longer

57

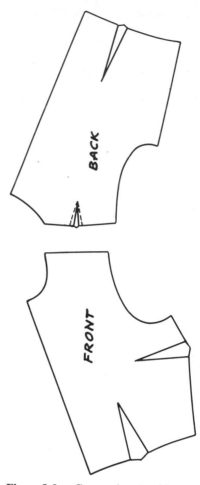

Figure 8-9.   Comparing shoulder seams

than the front. The average is about 3/8″ longer, but many people need more ease across the back. Remember, when you checked the front and back lengths of the bodice, you increased or decreased the bust dart to make them fit together. The same principle applies to the shoulder seam, but do *not* increase the shoulder darts until the front and back shoulder seams match exactly. Leave 3/8″ (or longer) of ease on the back shoulder seam. Some shoulders may need an extra shoulder dart—the individual who is very narrow across the front and wide across the back may add another one.

Your neckline and shoulder alterations now should be shaping up that fitting garment. These alterations are the most important because the shoulders act as a hanger. If the shoulder seams do not fit properly, the garment will not hang straight of grain. So check the shoulder seam location again—as you look straight ahead, the shoulder seam should sit 1″ behind your ear lobe (Figure 8-10). If it doesn't sit correctly, recheck your neckline and shoulder alterations.

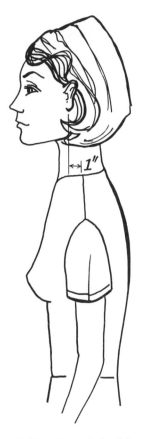

Figure 8-10.   Correct shoulder seam

9 *Armscye and Bust Dart Alterations*

ARMSCYE CHANGES

We sometimes overlook a very important area that helps in fitting the bustline—the armscye, or armhole. In Chapter 7 we talked of having only one armscye length. When you sit down, do your shoulder seams ride up? If so, do *not* take in the shoulder seams. You are short of scye. Fold out the extra length halfway of the armscye as shown in Figure 9-1.

Now the sleeve will not fit in, so take off half of this amount on the sleeve underarm. When the sleeve is set in, it should pivot slightly toward the front to hang straight of grain. It will hang straight of grain from top to elbow. Ignore the grain from the elbow down.

If you remove ½ ″ of front scye, decrease ¼ ″ from the front underarm, tapering to nothing at the wrist. But many times the woman who is short of scye is a C or D cup, and she needs extra fabric added at the front underarm. The amount folded out of scye

60

length is often added to scye width like this (in addition to her C cup alteration). If you add at the front underarm for larger cup measurement, you will not need to pivot the sleeve forward (see Figure 9-2).

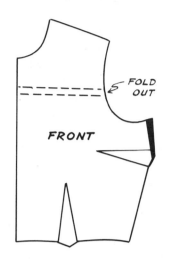

Figure 9-1.   Short scye and underarm width

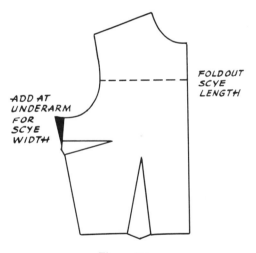

Figure 9-2.

BUST DARTS

In Chapter 6 we corrected the cup size, but what is in the cup may be in the wrong location. You must see "cloth on a body" to determine this—no amount of measuring will give you the *exact* location of the bust dart. Try the bodice on, pinned together at the center back with an accurate 5/8″ seam. Check in the mirror to be sure that the termination (end) of the bust dart points to the crest of the bust. Note that I said "points to," not "stops at"—there is a difference. Write down the amount you need to raise or lower the bust dart. The amount that the dart "stops short of" the crest of the bust is determined by the shape of the bust. If the dart termination extends beyond the crest, you are in a size pattern that is too large for you. (The bust that is very round on the side will have the dart stopping "shorter" of the crest. The dart will usually stop 1″ short of the crest of the bust. Do not change the length of the dart; this is *seldom* done. In fitting you delete the words "always" and "never.")

Raising the Bust Dart

If you have determined that the bust dart needs to be raised, measure up straight of grain from the termination (A in Figure 9-3), and connect the new termination back to B and C. You have raised the termination only—the amount was determined on your body.

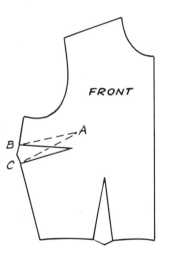

Figure 9-3.   Raising bust dart

Lowering the Bust Dart

For a slanted dart, this is simply a reverse procedure. Lower the termination the amount needed (A) and connect to B and C (Figure 9-4).

For straight of grain dart (Figure 9-5): if the bust dart on your pattern is slanted very little (most basic patterns give you a fairly straight dart), it is necessary to lower the entire dart. Measure down

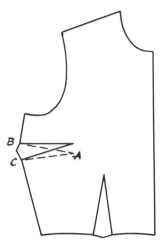

Figure 9-4. Lowering bust dart, slanted

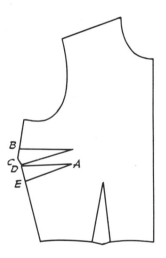

Figure 9-5. Lowering bust dart, straight of grain

straight of grain the amount needed and mark the new termination (A); then measure down from B to D and C to E. You have lowered the entire dart. The termination of a bust dart will never fall lower than straight of grain. You would look like your bra straps need tightening. (One of my students once told a neighbor that she was taking a fitting class and was learning to relocate the bust dart. Her neighbor's comment was: "You're paying money for that? I just tighten or loosen my bra straps!")

In the straight of grain dart method for lowering the bust dart, you must relocate the "jog" (the protrusion in a seam allowance caused when a dart interrupts the seam—see Fig. 9-6) Fold out in your pattern the new dart, then "true up" (or cut straight) from the underarm to the waist. Open out the pattern, and you have the new jog. (You will have cut off the old one.)

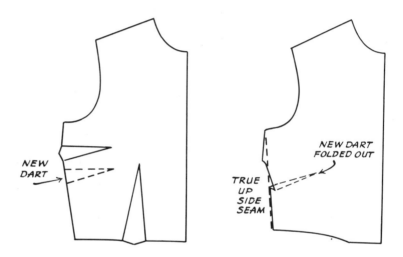

Figure 9-6.   Relocating jog in dart

10 *Sleeves*

If the shoulder area of your bodice has been altered correctly, many of your sleeve problems have been corrected also. You know that there is a reason for the sleeve being larger than the armscye, and it has to do with a good fit. The armscye is smaller and the more stationary side of the seam; the sleeve is where the action is and where you need the ease or fullness. So, do not take the ease out of the cap of a sleeve; you are simply eliminating a quality look as well as comfort.

CHANGING THE CAP

The grain on the sleeve will tell you your sleeve alteration. The sleeve grain lines should fall straight, but many times the horizontal or crosswise one pulls up, meaning that you need a longer cap. That alteration is done by adding more length to the cap (see Figure 10-1). Sometimes the vertical or lengthwise grain line is not hanging

65

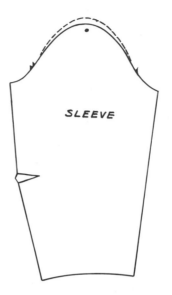

Figure 10-1. Adding to cap

straight. You will feel the sleeve hitting against the back of the arm; in other words, the arm is not falling in the middle of the sleeve. Simply redistribute the ease, by relocating the top of the sleeve at the shoulder seam.

If the sleeve grain lines are straight of grain, but the sleeve is too small, add to the underarm seams, tapering to nothing at the wrist. Note that if at any time you change the size of the armscye of the bodice, you must make the same alterations to the sleeve (or vice versa). (Figure 10-3).

Sometimes a sleeve ends up being actually larger than the armscye, but look at the figure. Is the individual "short of scye" with large arms? If so, ease the cap in as well as you can (grain lines straight), and nip the extra fullness in as a dart on the front underarm of the sleeve (Figure 10-4). Yes, it will look okay.

For a full upper arm, make an even fold across the cap of the sleeve above the notches. The width of the fold depends on the additional width needed in the cap. Cut the sleeve, continuing around the cap from the alteration fold about ½ " from the pattern edge of the sleeve cap (Figure 10-5). The sleeve cap will be 1 " wider and ½ " shorter (if 1 " was needed). It will fit the armscye perfectly.

If the upper part of the sleeve is hanging properly, check the location of the elbow darts (Figure 10-6). Fold your arm to your waist; the finished length should fall at the point where the hand ends and the wrist begins. With your arm still folded, mark (chalk or pin) the

Figure 10-2. The woman with muscular arms may need sleeve alterations.

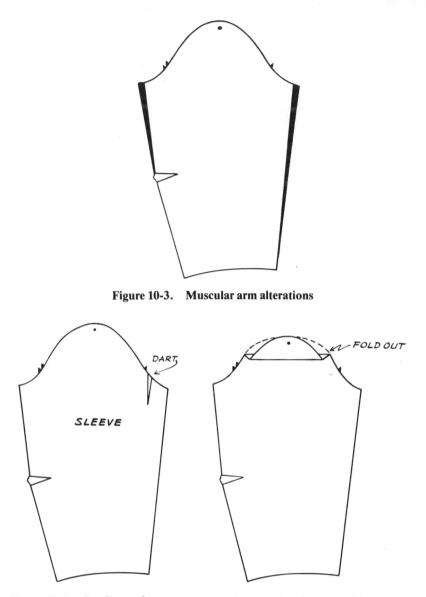

Figure 10-3. Muscular arm alterations

DART

SLEEVE

FOLD OUT

Figure 10-4. Small scye, large arm   **Figure 10-5. Shorter, wider cap**

sleeve as it hits the bend of the elbow. The darts point to the elbow. If they are low, shorten the girth or upper part of the sleeve by folding out the amount needed to raise the darts. (You may need to slash and insert a piece to lower the darts.) Then check sleeve length

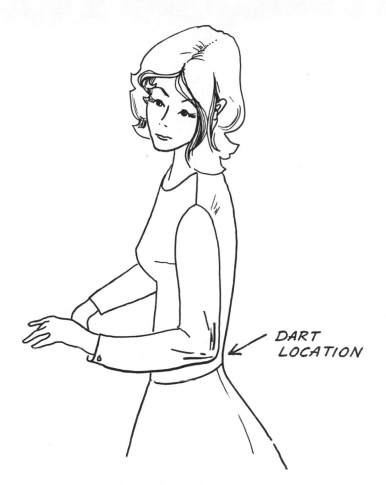

Figure 10-6.   Elbow dart location

and plus or minus to bottom edge (Figure 10-7). The sleeves should feel comfortable now. *But* do take care in setting in a sleeve. If it is not set in well, it will not fit comfortably.

There are many correct ways to set in a good-looking sleeve, but the flat method is the easiest way.

SETTING IN SLEEVES—FLAT METHOD

Stitch the shoulder seams of the garment. Be sure that you stitch from neck edge to shoulder, with the grain. Ease back shoulder to front. Put an ease line in the cap of the sleeve, stitching with a

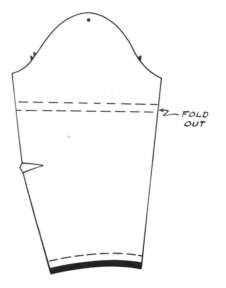

Figure 10-7. Sleeve length

regulation stitch for 2½ʺ from the underarm seam. Lengthen the stitch on the machine, and machine baste *on the seam allowance* around the cap of the sleeve, to 2½ʺ from the other underarm seam. Change to regulation stitch for the remainder of the seam. Stitch from right side of fabric; bobbin thread will be pulled for easing.

Clip the long stitch on the wrong side of the sleeve, at the beginning and end of the machine basting. Draw up the thread, adjusting the ease in the cap of the sleeve.

As you divide the cap of the sleeve in thirds, the most ease will be in the middle third, where the sleeve cap is greatest off-grain. There is no ease ½ʺ either side of the large dot at the top of the sleeve, where the fabric is straight of grain.

Place the sleeve on the bodice, right sides together, keying the notches of the sleeve to the armscye of the bodice. Match the dot at the top of the sleeve at the shoulder seam.

Extend the sleeve 3/8ʺ beyond the side seam of the bodice. This is ease at underarm. Begin to stitch 2½ʺ from the underarm seam, or where you started machine basting, around the cap of the sleeve to 2½ʺ from the underarm seam at the other side. Allow the sleeve to extend 3/8ʺ beyond the side seam of the bodice on this end also. Remember to hold the armscye firmly as you stitch, easing the cap of the sleeve into the armscye, following the line of ease stitching you did on the 5/8ʺ seam allowance. Press on the seam allowance, on the straight of grain, ½ʺ beyond the line of stitching.

Stitch the underarm seam of the bodice and the sleeve. Press both seams open. Complete the stitching of the sleeve, matching the underarm seams of the bodice and the sleeve, and overstitching for 1″ to be certain that the seam does not rip out. Trim the seam allowance to ½″.

Finish by pressing the remainder of the sleeve seam allowance over the end of a board or sleeve roll. Press it flat to the body of the garment. Note: Do not trim the armscye seam to more than ½″ and do not clip the seam, as you will be distorting the shape of the bodice.

Some alterations are easier to see on a short sleeve than a long one, so it is suggested that you make a fitting dress with one long sleeve and one short one. One student's husband took her picture in just such a dress, and mailed it to his mother to show how well the young lady's sewing was progressing!

Figure 10-8. ''Dear Mom: Betty is doing so well in sewing class . . .''

To complete your basic pattern, you must attach the bodice and skirt. You have the skirt on a tape, now you must ease the bodice onto the skirt. You were larger right below the waist, and you will be larger right above the waist. Pin the skirt and bodice, matching center front, center back, and side seams. Adjust waistline darts on the bodice by increasing or decreasing them as needed. Be sure to leave some ease on the bodice—do not nip the darts too tight. The bigger your "spare tire," the more ease you'll need.

Darts are made to fit your figure, and they will practically disappear if they really fit. The darts on your skirt will not match the darts on your bodice. Few women have busts that sit right over the hipbone, and those are the darts they usually try to match!

Some of you will have to relocate the waist darts, as well as increase or decrease them. The front waist darts must point to the crest of the bust, stopping short of the bust fullness.

Many figures look better without waistline darts. For a softer effect, use trouser pleats or gathers. I recommend locating darts on your fitting pattern, as you may want them for designing.

11 Using Your Basic Completed Pattern In General Sewing

CHECKING KEY AREAS

Once you have completed your fitting dress and find that your alterations are satisfactory, you are ready to begin to cut to fit. The fitting dress itself is now of little value to you, but the paper pattern you have created (your blueprint) is invaluable. Never cut up the fitting dress to use as a pattern. In fact, you will not even use your paper pattern to check out other patterns. (You may wish to cut your pattern in heavy paper or heavy weight pellon when you are sure of the fit.)

All garments have different construction and different silhouettes. To lay two patterns together and compare them will not get you the fit you want. You might write down your basic alterations in a little black book; they will be of more use to you than any pattern. Since patterns are standard, you will make the same alterations by the same amounts to all patterns (Vogue, Butterick, McCall's and Simplicity).

Figure 11-1.

One detail you may check from pattern to pattern is the bust dart (Figure 11-2). Generally speaking, if you raised or lowered the bust dart on the basic dress, you will do the same (by the same amount) on every garment before you cut it. To recheck—place your basic

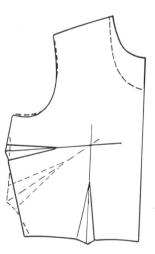

Figure 11-2.   Bust dart location

pattern under the pattern to be altered, keying together the center front and the natural shoulder seam. The bust darts may be a different angle, but they must point to the same crest of the bust.

Other areas you will need to check on every pattern are the hip measurement of a skirt and skirt length. Flat measure the hip area of each skirt because each designer gives a different amount of ease in each skirt. Cut to your personal "as you would like to wear it" measurement. Skirt lengths will vary not only in patterns, but certainly in fashion. Decide on a becoming length for your leg shape and body proportions, and, if necessary, vary it slightly to go along with current fashion.

Skirt darts will vary in number on each skirt. If you have three darts on the front of your basic skirt, you don't want every skirt to have three darts, and it isn't necessary. Instead of fitting a paper towel over a grapefruit, you might fit it on an overstuffed chair, (even if you don't look like one). It is a good place to learn to fit hip darts. The skirt darts point to your hipbone; the number will vary with each design, as will the amount of fabric allowed in the waist area. In Figure 11-3, one dart points to the hipbone); two darts sit on

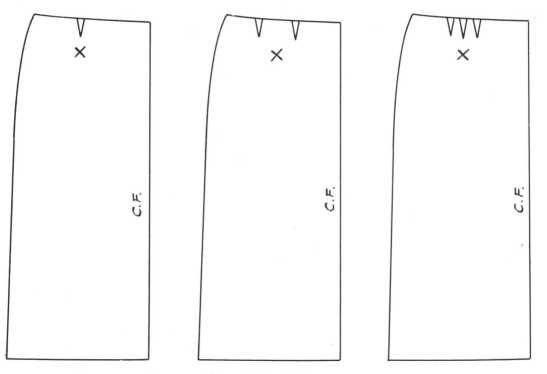

Figure 11-3. Hip darts

either side of the hipbone; and with three darts, the center one points directly to the hipbone, the others are one on each side.

Always locate darts by matching center front and center back together. Your darts will be located the same distance from the center front and center back on each skirt. Once your hip darts have been fitted correctly, they seldom, if ever, change location. Years may pass and even if you gain 20 pounds, your hipbone will not have moved. The darts will be in the same location, but the side seams will move out to enlarge the skirt.

It seems *too* simple to explain in these few paragraphs how to use the knowledge you have obtained by all the previous fittings. But once the fittings are over, you are truly ready to cut to fit. Think of all the time you are saving by not having to rip apart and restitch every other seam. Some people, including this author, follow a philosophy that says "if at first you don't succeed, quit." That is why this method of cutting to fit works for me, as it will for you.

Try your alterations on two or three "proof" dresses. You may want to vary the amount of the alteration. To stand and be fitted in a garment is quite different from wearing it. Check it with your lifestyle, and make sure it is comfortable. It may take more width across the back than you expected to hit that tennis ball or bid 4 no trump.

Figure 11-4.

12 *Using Your Basic Pattern for Designing*

When you are sure that you have a good fit, you can use your basic pattern to design. There are many books on flat pattern drafting, but here are just a few design ideas for the novice.

THE BASIC SKIRT

Your basic skirt may be an A-line or a "pencil-slim" straight skirt. Take your skirt *sloper* (as a designer you should know a little professional terminology—a sloper in the trade means a "basic pattern") and determine the amount of *flange* it has. (The flange is the flare on a skirt.)

A pencil-slim skirt would measure the same at the hem as at the hip area. The side seam from A to B (Figure 12-1) is perfectly straight of grain. The amount of flare from A to C or A to D is the

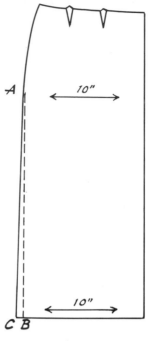

Figure 12-1.   Skirt flange

flange. From B to C is ¾ ", so this skirt (A to C) has a ¾ " flange. To flange, or flare, a skirt, add an equal amount front and back. Never decrease the flange on a pencil-slim skirt. The hem area must measure at least as much as the hip area. You might remember the peg skirts or harem skirts—very short-lived fashions because they were inconvenient. The hem area measured less than the hip in the peg and harem skirts, and you can imagine the difficulties with that. So make sure that the hem measures at least as much as the hip.

Eliminating Side Seam On Skirt

Make sure the side seam on your skirt sloper is straight of grain, no flange. Then simply overlap the side seams on the front and back from A to B (Figure 12-3). Lay the center front on the fold of the fabric, and cut just a center back seam. The upper part of what originally was the side seam now becomes a large dart terminating where the two side seam allowances cross each other, which is also the largest part of the hip. In stitching the dart, you will find it necessary to slash and trim before pressing it open. Stitch and press the other skirt darts toward center front and center back.

78

79 Figure 12-2. Harem skirt

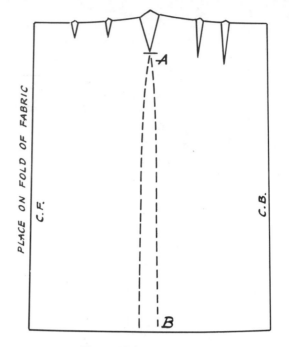

Figure 12-3.   No side seam

This skirt looks particularly good in plaids or large prints as it eliminates any matching (except the center back seam). It does require 54″ or 60″ fabric for many of us, but it also makes it possible for some to cut a skirt in one length of 45″ fabric (it usually takes two lengths). You have eliminated the two side seams (4 5/8″). Check your measurements, perhaps you can cut from 45″ fabric.

Pleats In Skirts

A skirt that is pleated all the way around is a difficult fitting problem, unless a commercial pattern fits your hips. You can pleat a piece of fabric and attach it to a yoke cut from your basic skirt pattern. Cut the yoke from the upper part of the skirt; the seam should hit at the largest part of your hip. When wearing an overblouse, it should cover the seam by 1″ at least. Turn and set the crease for the hem, and then make any size of pleats on a straight piece of fabric as shown (Figure 12-4). Attach the pleated section to the yoke. Note: The top of the pleated section must measure the same as the yoke at the hip seam.

Figure 12-4.   Pleats on a yoke

Figure 12-5.   Two side pleats

A few well-placed pleats are easy. For instance, take a piece of fabric your skirt cutting length, and press in the hem. Fold and set a couple of pleats. Place the basic skirt pattern over the pleats where you would like them to fall, perhaps over one leg. Cut out the basic skirt; it already has the pleats in it. Cut back as usual (Figure 12-5).

CONTOUR BELT

Would you like to make a contour belt that fits you perfectly? Simply use the top part of your basic skirt pattern as shown (Figure 12-6). Measurements may vary as to width. The skirt darts are folded out of the pattern before cutting. Cut from Pellon or heavy interfacing, and cover with fabric

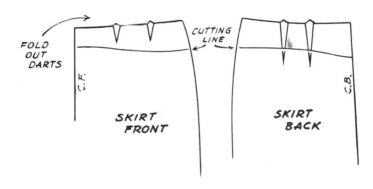

Figure 12-6.   Contour belt

DART CHANGES

Once you have the correct location and size of the bust dart on your basic pattern, you can relocate it anyplace. Shifting a dart to a new location does not alter the fit. To eliminate a waistline dart (for instance, not to interrupt a floral print), cut out the bust dart and the waist darts like pieces of pie. Continue to slash to the crest of the bust (A in Figure 12-7). Close up the waist dart, and it automatically makes the bust dart larger. Stitch the larger bust dart, using the termination of the original dart. Now there are no waistline darts at all and it fits you beautifully.

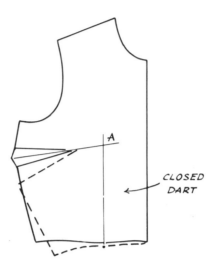

Figure 12-7.   Changing the bust dart

If you wish to eliminate the bust dart, but can use the waist dart (Figure 12-8), reverse the procedure. Close the bust dart and open the waistline dart more (Figure 12-9). Here is a great idea in a jersey—no bust dart and use the fabric from the waistline dart as soft gathers. No darts at all. This is also a good look for today's knits and soft fabrics, leaving plenty of room for your bustline.

The dart can be shifted to the armscye (Figure 12-10). This used to be found primarily in maternity clothes to accommodate the larger bust, but many fashionable dresses now carry this dart. Slash through the armscye to the crest of the bust, and close the bust dart. The armscye slash opens to form a dart (Figure 12-11).

A shoulder dart is flattering to lots of figures. Slash from halfway of shoulder to crest of the bust, and close up the bust and waist darts. The shoulder dart opens and may be stitched as a dart or as a soft pleat or gathers in jersey (Figures 12-12, 12-13). Be your own designer; let your fabric tell you what to do.

84

Figure 12-8.   Waistline darts

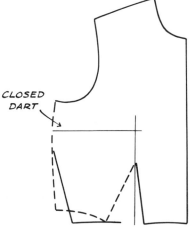

CLOSED
DART

Figure 12-9.   Changing the waistline dart

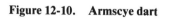

Figure 12-10.   Armscye dart

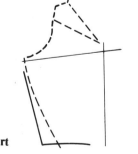

Figure 12-11.   Changing the armscye dart

Figure 12-12. Ease at shoulder

Figure 12-13. Changing the shoulder ease or dart

Many of you may like a long, slanted bust dart as opposed to the one on your basic. Slash at the angle you choose to the crest of the bust. Close the bust and waist darts, and the new dart opens. It will be quite large, so it will need to be trimmed out after stitching (Figures 12-14, 12-15). See Figure 9-6 on how to create the proper jog.

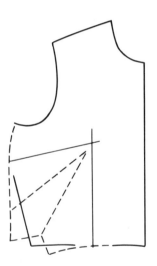

Figure 12-15.   Changing the slanted bust dart

Figure 12-14.   Slanted bust dart

Neckline darts as such are not too fashionable today, but gathers in soft jersey and crepes certainly are. Slash from the neckline to the crest of the bust. Close up the bust and waist darts; this opens a large

88

neckline dart. Cut a facing of your original neckline, then gather the fabric of the neckline dart to shaped facing (Figures 12-16, 12-17).

A center front dart is not the usual, but it is so flattering. Slash from center front seam to crest of the bust. Close the bust and waist

Figure 12-16.   Gathers at neckline

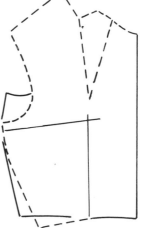

Figure 12-17.   Changing the neckline dart or ease

darts, and open the center front dart. This bodice in cutting requires a center front seam. The lower portion is cut straight of grain, causing the upper part to be bias. It fits beautifully (Figures 12-18, 12-19).

To cut your own princess line dress, slash the pattern in armscye A or shoulder B area (Figure 12-20) to crest of the bust. Close the bust dart only, leaving open the waist dart. Cut both sections apart and add a 5/8″ seam. Stitch together for the princess seam (Figure 12-21).

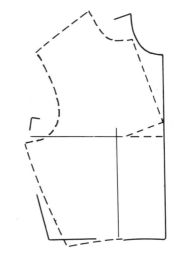

Figure 12-18.   Center front bust dart   **Figure 12-19.   Changing the center front dart**

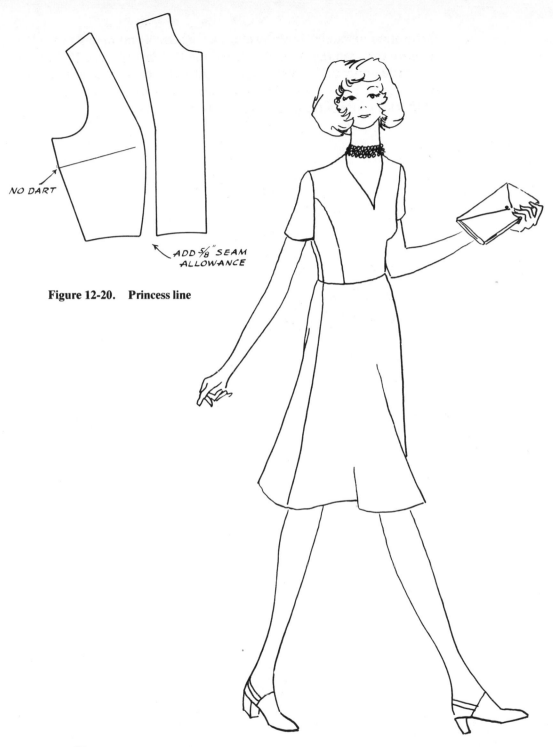

NO DART

ADD ⅝" SEAM
ALLOWANCE

Figure 12-20.   Princess line

91

Figure 12-21.   Princess seaming

Another attractive look by eliminating darts and placing the shaping into the seaming is done by slashing the dart (Figure 12-22). Cut apart the upper and lower bodice. Add 5/8″ seams, and stitch seams back together (Figure 12-23). Why not stitch tiny pin tucks in a piece of fabric before cutting the upper part of the bodice?

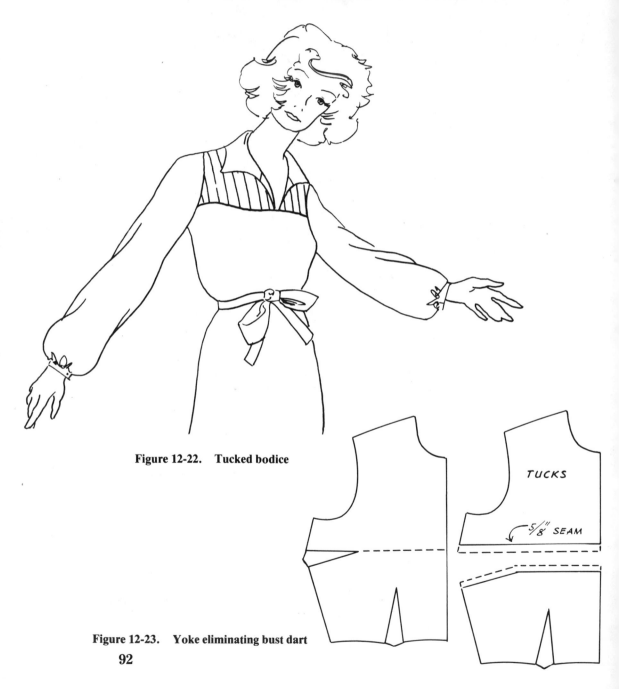

Figure 12-22.   Tucked bodice

Figure 12-23.   Yoke eliminating bust dart

13 *General Sewing Tips*

SLEEVES AND NECKLINES

Do you want to make a sleeveless dress from a pattern with sleeves? Don't just leave out the sleeve; your bra or slip will show. Instead, raise the armscye ½ ″ before cutting.

Do you want to set one sleeve into another dress pattern? Compare armscyes on the two bodices. If they are similiar in size and shape, you may interchange sleeve patterns. Don't try changing caps of sleeves. It is easier to change the shape of the armscye to go with your choice of sleeve.

Today's fashions show many patterns with no bust darts, but a good many of us need them. (You may get away without a bust dart if you are working in very soft sweater-like fabric or jersey.) To add a bust dart to a pattern that does not have one, you need your basic bodice pattern. Place tissue over it matching center front and natural shoulder seams. Transfer the bust dart to the tissue. Measure the size

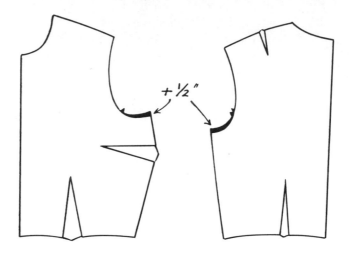

Figure 13-1. Sleeveless garment

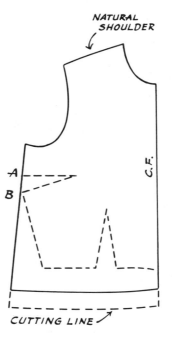

Figure 13-2. Adding bust darts

of your bust dart from A to B (Figure 13-2), and add that amount equally to the bottom of the front of the pattern. For instance, if the bust dart is 1½″ (A to B), add 1½″ to the bottom of the bodice all the way across the front. You may need to add extra paper to the pattern to cut jog in the dart (see Figure 9-6).

94

Are many designer patterns cut too low for you in the neckline? Once the dress is done, your only help is a large rose stuffed in the front (Figure 13-3). Why not correct the situation before it happens? Cut the neckline facings, baste the shoulder seams and try on the facing. Remember that the finished neckline will be 5/8″ lower once

Figure 13-3.

the seam is stitched. You may wish to turn under the neckline seam and baste in place. Alter the pattern neckline and cut new facings. Your only loss is in the facing, if it must be recut.

Something that often happens to a neckline is "gaposis" (Figure 13-4). First, are you sure that the back of the garment is wide enough

Figure 13-4. "Gaposis"

for you (see Figure 7-2 for total back width)? If it isn't, that could cause the front neckline to gap. This is difficult to determine by just a facing, so you may wish to cut the front of inexpensive fabric to try on. Then determine the amount of gap by folding out the excess at your neck edge. To alter the tissue pattern, take a fold (the determined amount) through the neckline of the bodice (Figure 13-5). Cut

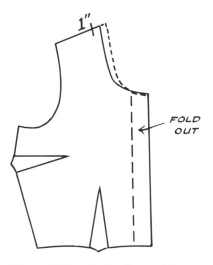

Figure 13-5.   Curing "gaposis"

out the new neckedge (true up the neckline free hand), turn the corner for 1″ unfold and cut the remainder of the bodice. You have widened the shoulder width only. This shoulder width may be narrowed as shown in Chap. 8, Fig. 8-18.

BASIC SILHOUETTES

The one piece shift dress has one major alteration totally different from the basic dress with waistline. If you check the plumb line of the shift, you find that many times the side seam swings to the front, and the dress is longer at the center back (Figure 13-6). To alter the finished dress, stitch out a pieshaped wedge of fabric at the back waistline. This seam could be covered with a belt.

To cut to fit a shift dress, you need to know the size of that wedge; this is the same amount the side seam swings to the front. The alteration is actually the opposite of the dowager curve (see Figure 8-6). Drop the neckline the amount needed and trace the identical neckline; turn corner to A and true up shoulder to B. You are actual-

98   **Figure 13-6. Shift dress, not plumb**

SHIFT
SLOPER

Figure 13-7. Shift dress

ly cutting the wedge from the shoulder area, and you're plumb (Figure 13-7)!

An interesting note on the shift dress, is how it came into fashion. Many, many years ago, this silhouette was called a chemise and used as an undergarment only. In the 1950s, designers introduced the sack dress. The name in itself spelled disaster, and it *was* one of the biggest disasters in retail history. At that time women were wearing clothes very similar to the basic dress—fitted, close-to-the-body garments. The sack was a too-sudden change. But about 10 years later, the shift dress was introduced and was an immediate success; in fact, it has become a classic. It's all in the timing. The silhouettes were the same, but women were now ready for such a change. Soft-gathered bodices and eased skirts slowly got us ready for the shift.

Another silhouette is the garment with a cut-on sleeve—kimono, dolman, raglan. It has a deep armscye and a winglike silhouette (Figure 13-8). It retains none of the under armscye curve of the nor-

Figure 13-8. Cut-on sleeve

mal set-in sleeve. The alterations for this design are similar to the basic dress. Figures 13-9 through 13-14 show how to adapt the basic dress alterations to the cut-on sleeve. The individual with narrow, sloping shoulders should not use this design. It requires at least average width shoulders to support the fabric of the cut-in-one bodice.

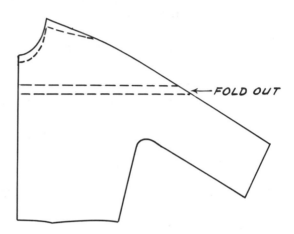

Figure 13-9. Short of scye

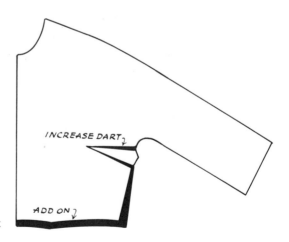

100   **Figure 13-10. Large bust**

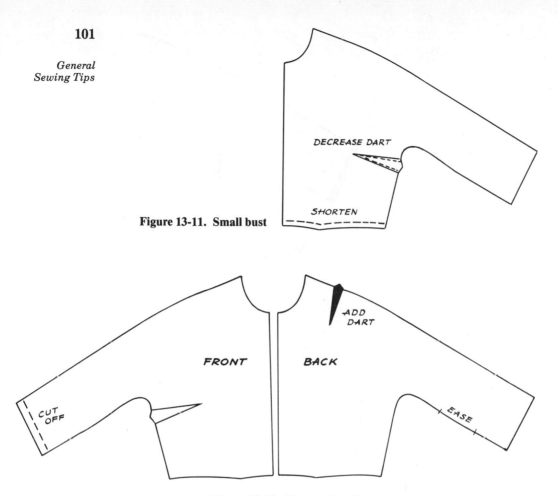

Figure 13-11. Small bust

Figure 13-12. Narrow shoulders

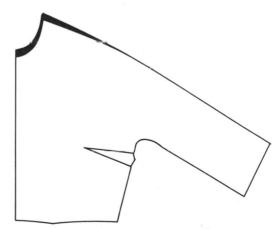

**Figure 13-13. Fullness at front
neck, or dowager done on back.**

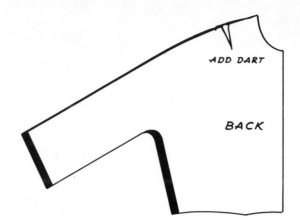

Figure 13-14. Total width

14 *Altering for the Large Woman*

Of course, this chapter is not for *you,* but you may have a *friend* who is slightly overweight or large. Actually, this chapter is not only for overweight women, but also for the larger woman whose fitting problems are not related to weight. We all know how much better we look and feel when our clothes fit properly; no one knows this better than the larger woman. Pattern companies usually forget the larger figure and project their patterns for average size. Understandably, it's a matter of economics. But for the larger woman that may mean making a dress with no style and poor fit. She wants to be, and can be, just as fashionable as her smaller, thinner sister.

Pattern companies grade commercial patterns by increasing length as they increase width. Many times this is not the solution for the larger woman. She may be short in stature. Many women will require a larger size pattern in the front than the back, or vice versa. For instance, the woman with the large bust often has a small, very straight back.

Figure 14-1.   Taste makes *waist*

It does require experience and skill in altering a complicated design. It would be easier for the larger woman to buy her fitting pattern and do the alterations she needs as suggested in this text. Then she can use her basic pattern to make simple changes as I suggested in Chapter 12.

COMMON ALTERATIONS

Following are some alterations common to the larger woman.

Dowager Curve (see also Chapter 8)

Many times a heavy bust pulls the shoulders forward, causing a need for this alteration in the back (Figure 14-2).

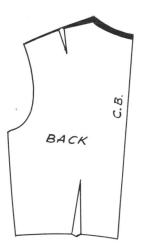

Figure 14-2.   Dowager curve alteration for the larger woman

Stomach and Waistline

The round, barrel front is covered stylishly by the alteration in Figure 14-3. Add by cutting straighter of grain across the waistline of the skirt; you will probably need to add at the waistline from the hip up as well. Front darts are seldom required on this figure type; use soft ease instead. The alteration of cutting straighter of grain at the waistline also may be used on the back for the figure that carries a "spare tire" right below the waistline in the back.

Figure 14-3.   Large stomach and waist

Bodice Alterations

Bodice alterations were covered in Chapters 6 through 10, but often the larger woman needs even more help. If the C cup alteration was not enough to cover, she may need additional fabric. (The bodice will pull across the armscye and upper arm.) In addition to the C cup alteration, add an extra amount at the underarm, then add the same amount to the sleeve (Figure 14-4). This accommodates the larger bust and larger arm. You also may wish to raise the armscye another ½" at the underarm. This eliminates dragline or fold that falls diagonally at the armscye.

The larger bust will require a larger dart. The rounded figure needs two or three darts, the flatter figure, one large dart. The larger busted figure also will do well to have a shallower armscye and be cut longer at the underarm.

Sleeves

Sleeves present a problem for the larger woman, and if they were not covered adequately for you in Chapter 10, remember these few things. Often the only thing wrong with your sleeve is improper distribution of ease due to body contour or bone structure, so don't be afraid to change the shoulder seam location on the cap of the sleeve. Moving it ½" one way or the other is often the solution. If

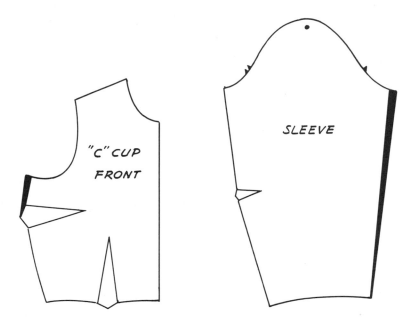

Figure 14-4.   Bodice alterations for C cup and larger

the circle of the armscye seems small, add to the shoulder or underarm seam; do not cut armscye deeper.

Increasing

To increase a pattern by one size, simply give total width (3/8" per size) to front and back (Figure 14-5). Many times you like the style of a pattern, but it doesn't run large enough.

MATERNITY CLOTHES

Pattern companies often neglect another type of larger woman—the mother-to-be. It is essential to a pregnant woman's health that her clothes move when she does and never bind anywhere. It's said that pregnant women have a special glowing beauty, but when you're 8½ months and carrying 35 extra pounds, it's not easy to feel pretty. Wearing pretty clothes that fit can help.

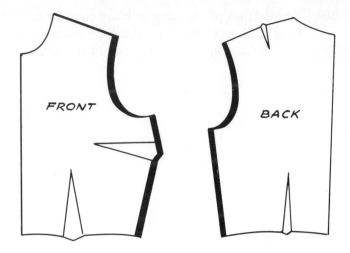

Figure 14-5.   Giving total width

Figure 14-6.   Just waiting

You may decide to use just one or two maternity patterns and vary them with details—change necklines, add sleeves, trims, and so on. Don't get too fussy; keep the lines simple. Many of your regular patterns can be altered simply by adding to the side seams and increasing the bust darts. Your neckline and shoulders will not change in pregnancy.

Usually the additional amount is needed on the front only although you may need to add a little to the hip area in the back. The amount you add depends on which month you are in and how strict your doctor is about diet. Do some measuring, but leave room for expansion (Figure 14-7).

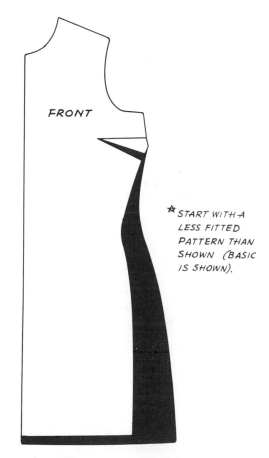

FRONT

✱ *START WITH A
LESS FITTED
PATTERN THAN
SHOWN (BASIC
IS SHOWN).*

Figure 14-7.   Maternity wear

15 *Line and Design*

Too many people who sew have garments that *look* like they made them. . . . that "fireside touch". The dress may have a perfect zipper, perfectly stitched seams, and beautifully eased sleeves, but it still lacks professionalism. Usually the fault is the choice of fabric and pattern. The classroom has overstressed technique and forgotten "chic."

CHOICE OF FABRIC

Picture the girl who made the designer dress in a cotton print, and covered the buttons and belt with matching fabric—beautiful construction, but poor choice of goods. Or the one who added hat, scarf, and purse to match (Figure 15-1)! Use quality fabric when you sew; your time is too valuable to spend on cheap cloth. All the workmanship in the world can't do much with cheap fabric. A good quality fabric, the simplest pattern, a purchased belt—the image

110

Figure 15-1.

might even overshadow the not-so-well-set-in sleeve. To achieve the chic, you also must know what silhouette or line is best for your figure type.

SEWING FOR FIGURE TYPE

Choosing the correct pattern or design for your body is a study of proportion and balance. If you have had any art classes, you will find pattern choice a lot easier. But even without art training, you can improve your selections. Proportion means that all areas of your body are related and flow in an easy visual line. Balance gives an equal amount of interest or emphasis in each direction. Balance is usually achieved by dramatizing one detail of an outfit; understatement in an outfit means elegance. Don't overdo the emphasis.

With the correct use of line, design, and proportion, you can create an illusion of *natural* perfection, at the same time making your own fashion statement. Your fashion image makes the distinction. "Clothes make the man or woman" or "You are what you wear".

At the beginning of this book, you were asked how you saw yourself. If you see yourself as tall, thin, long-legged, and ever so svelte you don't need any help. But if the picture was something else, let's face reality, but pursue the dream.

Bone structure is the most important thing to note as you study your anatomy. Flesh can be moved around, added on, and taken off, but the bone structure is yours. Use it to its best advantage. The shoulder bone acts as a hanger for all garments. The more flesh added to your bone structure, the more support to your fabric. But if too much flesh has been added, it causes a distortion.

If your body is too thin or slight, it causes the fabric to wrinkle and sag from lack of support. These are problem areas not to be accented. In choosing a pattern, minimize problem areas through appropriate choice of design line. Sew to enhance your assets.

The ideal figure has a prominent bone structure with ample but firm flesh and muscle producing contoured areas in pleasing proportions. The ideal figure measures the same width across the front shoulders as the hip.

Let's work with our assets, or make them work for us, certainly a more "fun" approach than working with our problems.

112

Figure 15-2. How do you see yourself?

Line is really the style of the garment. Strategically placed seaming gives lines, as does the silhouette. The lines of your clothes produce movement, causing the eye to move in different directions—vertical, horizontal, diagonal. With these design lines, you should direct the eye to your assets and away from your problem areas.

In the following illustrations, note that your eye follows the direction of a line, the most dominant line.

1. Vertical lines seem to add height, to give a feeling of simplicity and dignity (like the towering skyscraper (Figure 15-3). One vertical seam at the center front gives a taller, thinner look than two seams running up and down. With two seams, your eye runs across the figure to the second seam.

2. Horizontal lines add width (Figure 15-4), but give a feeling of calmness and repose (like the horizon itself). Use horizontal lines at meager areas to balance out substantial areas. For instance, use a yoke seam above a meager bust to balance out substantial hips. To divide one's figure in half horizontally is not flattering, a ⅓, ⅔, or ¼ division is more interesting. "Chubbies" should not have vertical or horizontal lines in a dress. The emphasis should be within the silhouette.

3. Long diagonals give height, short ones often cause the eye to travel horizontally (Figure 15-5). Diagonal lines add grace and tend to slim the figure.

If you have too much curve to your figure, don't add another. Curved seaming will add roundness and weight where it falls on your figure. Remember—your use of line should be dictated by your own body type.

Not to say you can't use some of these line directions, just don't make them the main focal point. There are exceptions to every rule, as you know your own figure you can adapt and alter the rules. It is not possible in any one book to list all the do's and don't's of dressing for your figure type. None of the rules work alone; they interact with each other to give a pleasing appearance. You *must* know yourself.

Next to bone structure, the most obvious thing to note as you study yourself is your height. You can probably fit yourself into either tall or short—few are "average." A woman of 5′6″ would be

about average, but if she is a little heavy she should dress as the short

Figure 15-3.   Vertical lines

Figure 15-4.　Horizontal lines

116

Figure 15-5. Diagonal lines

girl, and if she is a little underweight she should dress as the taller girl. She also could be average in height, heavy in the hips, and meager in the bust. So, here we are back to proportion and balance.

If you are tall, you have many advantages and can give a fashion model image. Depending upon weight, you can be more dramatic with fabric and design lines. Dress in scale to your size, no tiny prints, collars, or accessories. However, if you wish to appear shorter, cut your height with horizontal lines. Contrast yokes, belts, and other accessories.

117   If you are short and quite thin, you have few limitations to what

you can wear. But dress in scale, no large prints, large hats, or full, full skirts. They bury you! Use vertical design lines and one color dressing from head to toe if you want a slimmer, leaner look. Long cigarette sleeves, V-necklines, and vertical closures are becoming.

EMPHASIS

Bust, waist, hips, and shoulders are the areas you will wish to emphasize or de-emphasize with design lines. To emphasize shoulder areas, wear raglan sleeves, set-in sleeves, or sleeveless and yoke construction. They will draw the eye to the shoulder area. *However,* If you have narrow shoulders, stay away from dolman and raglan sleeves.

If you have a hollow chest, do not wear sleeveless garments. The fabric will hang loosely, and the armscye will appear too large and gap.

Always keep the bust in proportion to the hips. If you wish to enlarge or emphasize the bust, wear the following—low necklines, cowl necklines, yokes, or an empire waist if you have some length in the rib cage. A set-in sleeve minimizes the bust.

If your waist presents a pleasing proportion, accent it with belted garments, and wear short jackets and vests. If you have a large waist, minimize it by creating vertical lines on your body.

The hip area supports skirts and pants. If the hipline is well padded, the flesh gives the support, not the bone. If your hips are large, emphasize the bust. Wear collars, pockets, yokes, and details above the waist. To emphasize hips, wear long jackets cut at the hipbone.

A large number of American women need to de-emphasize their hips. The most slimming skirt fits well in the torso or hip area; it could have flare below that, a pleat or a wrap. All-around pleated skirts add some bulk to hips, as do heavily gathered skirts. The less fabric in the hip area, the better you look.

Skirt lengths have been said to rise and fall with the stock market. Fashion should not really dictate length (although it usually does). You should wear what looks best on you. Your skirt should skim or stop at the curve of your calf; the legs will then taper gracefully from hemline to ankles (see Figure 15-6). This skirt length is a true leg lengthener for everyone. All of your skirts need not be the exact length, vary them ½ " with style. Straight skirts look better longer. Shorten a fuller skirt, particularly in a lightweight fabric.

Unless you are tall, a jacket that comes well below the hip can make you look like you're standing in a hole. A jacket that stops just

Figure 15-6.   Flattering skirt length

above the fullest part of your hip is flattering; it can be longer with pants.

A wrap coat lengthens your figure—but not too much wrap. Too much fabric adds pounds.

These guidelines can help you to think about your figure type. Use the ideas, modify them, adapt them to your figure. Try on clothes from your own closet, and study the design lines. Why is that blue dress your favorite? Because it's comfortable and fits well? Flattering design lines? Or is it the color?

COLOR AND SEWING

You respond to form (line and design) with your mind and to color with your emotions. Color can create your mood. It raises or lowers your spirit, warms or cools your heart, or can cause great excitement. Certain colors emphasize or camouflage. Some recede or advance. You express your own personality in the colors you wear.

Looking at the color wheel (Figure 15-7), let's begin at the top with yellow, the lightest color, expressing cheer, fun, and gaiety. Moving clockwise, green, the jungle or forest color (nature) gives a restful feeling. Bluegreen denotes a cool, calm, peaceful existence. Blue is subduing—dignity, poise, reserve. (In paintings of madonna and child by the old masters, the Virgin's robe is always blue; this serene color is part of her.) Blue-violet, or fuschia, is a bit stimulating, and purple is the color of royalty. Majestic wealth comes to mind, although it is also said that purple is depressing. From yellow to purple on the wheel has been a down movement, both directionally and psychologically. Things pick up as we move past red-violet, or shocking pink. Red is exciting, the color of love and passion. It speeds things up. Orange is an activating color, often worn by those who are very sociable. From red-violet upward to the yellow, all colors are stimulating, exciting, and even aggressive. They can increase pulse rate, heartbeat, and respiration. They are the warm, advancing colors.

Studies in California and Texas suggest that Westerners really do prefer bright sunny colors (often called California colors). Colors that remind them of desert flowers. Maybe its because one has to use bold, bright colors to make any kind of impression on the vast landscape.

What does color have to do with fitting? Two identical garments in different colors will seem to fit differently. The eye is attracted to light, bright colors, making that area appear larger. Some people advocate fitting the light, bright, warm color garment closer to the figure to counteract the force of color. Light, bright, warm, advancing colors make the figure look heavier. Grayed, dark, cool, receding colors make it look slimmer. Light colors reflect light, and dark colors absorb it. In the summer, we wear light colors; they not only appear cooler, they are cooler. Dark (winter) colors appear warmer, and they actually are.

Make color work to enhance your figure type. Wear the dark, cool colors if you wish to look slimmer. If you wish to add weight to a meager figure, wear bright, warm colors. For instance, you may look quite heavy in a white dress, but if you wear a black dress, a friend may ask if you've lost weight. You would think we'd see more people in black for that reason alone, but many say they can't wear it. Just remember that black worn next to the face requires more makeup; the black has robbed the face of color. And in choosing a

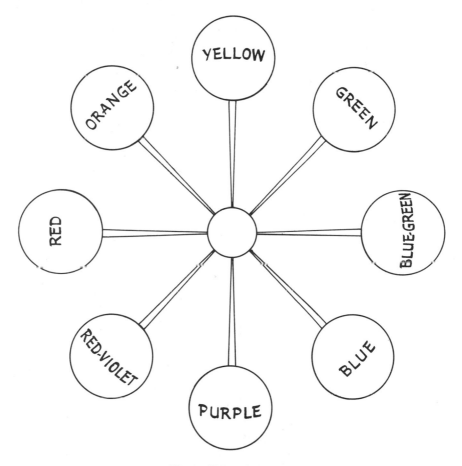

Figure 15-7.   Color wheel

black fabric, choose a good one—not a brown or grayed black. Silk takes the best dye and gives you the truest black. Black is considered mysterious and somber, rich and dignified. Wear it, but change your makeup.

Whatever color you wear, you are going to look better—because now you have that "perfect fit!"

Figure 15-8.

MEASUREMENT CHART

PERSONAL		PATTERN	+ OR –
Waist (band) measurement	_____	Waist measurement (as stated on pattern according to size) _____	_____
Hip measurement (as you would like to wear it)	_____	Hip measurement (flat measurement) _____	_____
Skirt length　　　Finished	_____	Skirt length (cutting) _____	_____
Hem (+2½)	_____		
Cutting length	_____		
Front bodice length	_____	Bodice length _____	_____
Back bodice length	_____	Bodice length _____	_____

Index

A

Alterations:
  armscye, 45-46 *(fig.)*, 60-61 *(fig.)*, 93, 94 *(fig.)*
  back, 47 *(fig.)*
  bodice, 41-44
  bust darts, 62 *(fig.)*, 63 *(fig.)*, 64 *(fig.)*
  front, 47, 50 *(fig.)*, 51
  neckline, 52, 54 *(fig.)*
  shoulder, 55, 56 *(fig.)*, 57 *(fig.)*, 58 *(fig.)*, 59
  sleeves, 65-66 *(fig.)*, 67 *(fig.)*, 68
    length of, 70 *(fig.)*
Armhole (*see* Armscye)
Armscye, 9, 44, 45, 52, 54, 55, 70, 71, 100, 106, 107
  alterations of, 45-46 *(fig.)*, 60-61 *(fig.)*, 93, 94 *(fig.)*

Index   Back, 35, 103
   alterations of, 46-47 *(fig.)*
Basting, 28
Belt, contour, 82, 84 *(fig.)*
Bodice, 7, 8, 27, 70
   alterations, 41-44
     of bra cups, 43-44
     of length, 50 *(fig.)*, 51
     practicing of, 41
   joining to skirt, 72
   measuring, 47
   tucked, 92 *(fig.)*
Bones, structure, 112, 114
Bra, 5, 6, 7
   cups, 5
     alterations of, 43 *(fig.)*, 44 *(fig.)*
Bubble, 9
Bust, 4, 5, 6, 7, 8, 9, 103, 114, 118
   relation to size, 6
   size, alterations of, 6, 41-44

C

"Chic," 110, 111
Color,
   choice of, 120-22
   effects of, 120
   and figure, 120-21
   and seasons, 121
Cups, bra *(see* Bra, cups)
Cutting, to fit, 12, 14

D

Darts, 9, 28, 38, 39, 43, 47, 58, 68, 72, 78
   adding to bust, 94 *(fig.)*
   armscye, 82, 85 *(fig.)*
   bust, 61-62, 87 *(fig.)*, 89 *(fig.)*
     alterations of, 62-64, 93-94 *(fig.)*

Darts (cont.)
    changes in, 82, 84-85 *(figs.)*, 86-87 *(figs.)*, 89-90
    eliminating, 90, 92 *(fig.)*
    front, 90 *(fig.)*
    hips, 75-76 *(figs.)*
    neckline, 87, 88 *(fig.)*
    shoulder, 82
    waistline, 84 *(fig.)*, 85 *(fig.)*
Derrière, 9
    alterations of, 36 *(fig.)*
    flat, 35
    protruding, 35
Diagonals *(see* Lines, diagonal)
Dolman *(see* Sleeve, cut-on)
Dowager curve, 54
    alterations of, 105
Dresses:
    princess line, 89, 90-91 *(figs.)*
    shift, 97, 98 *(fig.)*, 99 *(fig.)*
    sleeveless, 93
    strapless, 93

E

Ease, 8, 9,
Elbow, 68, 69
    darts in, 68

F

Fabric:
    blocking, 24, 26, 27
    cheap, 110
    choice of, 110
    cutting lengths, 27 *(fig.)*
    grain *(see* Grain)
    straightening, 26 *(fig.)*
Figure, 112, 114, 117-18 *(see also* Fit)
Figure type:
    self-assessment, 112, 114
    sewing for, 112

Fit, 8-11
    bust, 9
    to figure, 9-10
    skirt, 9
    sleeves, 9
    waist, 9
Flange:
    of skirt, 77-78 *(figs.)*
Flare
    (see Flange*)*

G

"Gaposis," 96-97 *(figs.)*
Girdle, 32, 34
Grading, 7
Grain, fabric, 10, 12, 24, 27, 28, 38, 39, 54, 66, 77
    lines, 13 *(fig.)*

H

Height:
    effect on choice of lines, 114, 117-18
Hem, 35, 78
Hips, 6, 9, 20, 32, 38, 40, 114, 118
    darts, 75 *(fig.)*, 76
    high, 18, 34
    measuring, 15, 16 *(fig.)*
Horizontals *(see* Lines, horizontal)

J

Jacket, 118, 120

K

Kimono *(see* Sleeve, cut-on)

Lines, 114
    diagonal, 114, 115 *(fig.)*
    horizontal, 114, 116 *(fig.)*
    vertical, 114, 117 *(fig.)*

M

Maternity, 107
    alterations for, 108 *(fig.)*, 109 *(fig.)*
Measuring self, 4–6, 9, 14-15
Measurements, flat,
    for skirt, 15, 18

N

Neckline:
    alterations of, 52, 54-55, 97
    facings for, 96
    "gaposis" of (*see* "Gaposis")
    gathers at, 88 *(fig.)*

O

"Off grain," (*see* Grain)
Overweight:
    alterations for, 103
        bodice, 106, 107 *(fig.)*
        dowager curve, 105 *(fig.)*
        sleeves, 106-07 *(fig.)*
        stomach, 105
        waistline, 105, 106 *(fig.)*

P

Panty hose, 32
Paper, 73

Pattern companies:
    Butterick, 4, 74
    McCall's, 4, 74
    Simplicity, 4, 74
    Vogue, 4, 74
Patterns, 3-4, 5-7, 43-44
    use in designing, 77-92
    use in sewing, 73-76
"Pencil-slim" (*see* Skirt, A-line)
Pleats, 72
    in skirts, 80, 81 *(fig.)*, 82, 83 *(fig.)*
"Plumb," definition, 35
"Plumb lines, correction of, 36 *(fig.)*, 39-40
Pressure gauge, 30

R

Raglan (*see* Sleeve, cut-on)
Ready to wear, 3 (*see also* Sizes)

S

Seam, 24
    back, 34
      of skirt, 29
    eliminating, 78
    front, 58, 59
    princess, 91 *(fig.)*
    shoulders, 58, 59
    side, 35, 76, 77
    underarm, 44, 70
Selvage, 26
"Sew buddy," 32
Sewing machine, use of, 30
Shoulder, 54, 101
    alterations for, 55, 57-59
    emphasis in design, 118
    high, 18
Shrinkage, 29
Silhouettes, basic (*see* Dress, shift)

Size, 3-7
    determining, 4-5 *(fig.)*, 6 *(fig.)*, 7 *(table)*
    half size, 7
    increasing, 107
    Misses Petite, 7
    patterns, 3, 4
    ready to wear, 3
    standardization of, 3, 4
Skirt, 6, 8, 9, 14-15, 18, 38, 51, 76
   A-line, 77
   alterations of, 19 *(fig.)*, 20-23, 21 *(fig.)*
   construction of, 28-31
   fitting of, 32-40
   length, 75, 118
   personal length, 15, 17 *(fig.)*
   self-measurement for, 14-15
   taping, 29-31, 29 *(fig.)*
   tummy, altering, 39 *(fig.)*
   waistline, altering, 22 *(fig.)*, 23 *(fig.)*, 40 *(fig.)*
Sleeves, 9, 52, 55, 118
   alterations of, 65-68
   caps of, 65-66
     alterations to, 65, 66 *(fig.)*
   cut-on, alterations of, 101-02 *(fig.)*
   overweight, 106-07 *(fig.)*
   setting in,
     flat method, 69-71
Sloper (skirt), 77
Stay stitch, 25 *(fig.)*, 51, 52 *(fig.)*
Symmetry, lack of in body, 18
   allowing for lack, 18

T

Taping, 29-31

V

Verticals (*see* Lines, vertical)

Index

Waist, 9, 14, 20, 22, 29, 47, 118
    altering, 51
    overweight, 105
Weight,
    effect on choice of lines, 114, 117-18

Y

Yoke, 80, 92 *(fig.)*, 114, 118

Z

Zipper, 28